ANNIHILATING ANOREXIA

A MEMOIR

MICHELE MASON

THE PAPER HOUSE
PUBLISHING

To all of you who have Anorexia. May you find something in these pages to help you annihilate it. You deserve a beautiful, healthy, happy life.

And to Grandma Mason, my North Star

Let me feel all I need to feel in order to heal.

Let me heal all I need to heal in order to feel.

-Anonymous

CONTENTS

PROLOGUE: REPAIRS AND RECRIMINATIONS

My bathing suit was ripped. Looked like the seam came apart in the back. If I put it on, I'd be exposing my bare bottom, and the rip would probably get even bigger. The suit was a one-piece and made out of cheap material in a bright lime green color. It was the beginning of summer in 1973.

The setting for most of my story is Erie, Pennsylvania (PA). During the summers, there were plenty of opportunities to go to the beaches at Presque Isle, which is a peninsula on Lake Erie. There were also family weekends spent at the local campground, and the campground had a swimming pool. No way was I going to get through the summer without a bathing suit.

I had to fix it. Why? It made me anxious that it ripped. Anxiety was a familiar emotional friend. It was a constant companion that seemed to hang around more and more throughout my childhood. I was the eight-year-old middle child in our traditional family of dad, mom, and three kids. My parents, Marty and Sylvia, started having kids in 1962 when they were both only 20 years old. Five years later, all three of us were here. I was the only girl.

If I could fix my bathing suit, that would solve a problem. I could avoid creating drama that would arise if I asked my parents for a new bathing suit. We didn't have the money for frivolous things like new clothes every summer. I laid the suit out on my bed, and went to the closet in the hallway to get the sewing things my mother, Sylvia (Sly for short) kept there in a tin box.

Not sure how I learned to use a needle and thread at just eight years of age, but on this particular afternoon, the knowledge would definitely come in handy. Since the suit was lime green, it was unlikely I would find a lime green thread to match exactly, so I used black thread. I threaded the needle, turned the suit inside out, and proceeded to sew up the seam. I took great care to make sure any messy stitches only showed on the inside of the suit. On the outside of the suit, only small bits of the black thread would show, which should be okay.

I took my time with the task. Again, I didn't want to have to ask my parents to buy me a new suit. It would make me feel guilty, plus the same old anxiety. The reason it would make me feel guilty is because whenever money was spent on anything is our household, Sly would react negatively. The dysfunction she had with money would condition me to feel bad about wanting things that cost money, no matter the amount. I grew to believe I didn't deserve new things, even if they were necessities.

In reality, of course, the beliefs I started developing at such a young age were false. Sly was just thrifty to the extreme. She had pancakes of old makeup scattered on her dresser. The bottles were left open, with liquids and powders spilled directly on the wood surface of the dresser. It was a mess. She had dozens of cheap plastic shoes from the thrift shop. They were piled up in the closet and under the bed with a thick layer of dust on them.

I needed to get the maximum wear out of the clothes I had. There was an insinuation in our household that I was privileged because I was the only girl. I didn't have to wear hand-me-downs like my younger brother did. Yes, my clothes were new when I got them, but they were of cheap quality. I wore them until I grew out of them. The few cotton dresses I had for the summer of my eighth year would become the shirts I wore in the summer of my ninth year. Money was a source of great contention between my parents. Sly was an extreme saver and Marty was an extreme spender. Opposites attract, perhaps? We were straight up, middle working class like most people in Erie. Money was meant for school, food, gas, electricity, and the mortgage. Just the essentials; no luxuries allowed. Certainly not a new bathing suit, when I already had one.

Taking all of this into consideration, I tried to ratchet down my anxiety. I would rather make my best effort at sewing the rip in the suit. I didn't dare approach my parents. No money required, just a needle, thread, and little bit of time. Once the mending job was finished, I turned the suit back to right side out. I held it up and admired my work. I tried it on, and the stitches seemed to hold up. My plan worked! No one would know it ripped, and I had a suit that would be good for another summer. I removed it, laid it carefully back on the bed, and put my regular play clothes back on. I was very pleased with myself.

As I was putting the sewing things away, Sly walked by my bedroom, and stopped to see what I was doing. I said "Look, mom, I fixed my bathing suit!" Sly picked up the suit, glanced at the repair work, and rolled her eyes. She threw it on the floor, let out a loud, exaggerated sigh, gave me a look of utter exasperation, and walked out of the room.

What? Are you kidding me? This was not the response I was expecting. My eight-year-old self knew there was something wrong about her negative response, but I didn't know what it was. All of the positive thoughts that went through my brain while I was doing the repair job disappeared in a nanosecond. Yet another example of how my positivity was being snuffed out, slowly and painfully. Her verbal lashing always felt worse than the occasional physical beatings I got. The physical reaction started to kick in. Pain in my gut. Tightness in my chest. I willed myself *not* to cry. If I cried, she might come back and hit me. She didn't want to deal with a crying child. She didn't want to deal with me.

She had a habit of walking away immediately after her negative comment or gesture. I think it was intentional. What you might call a flame thrower. She excelled at this. When she walked away abruptly and quickly, she made it impossible for me to respond. Instead, I got to sit with the impact her words and actions had on me. I got to internalize the big emotions of confusion, hurt, disappointment, and anger. All of it contributing to the anxiety, which was like a snowball rolling down the hill; it just got bigger and rolled faster. My anxiety loved association. Every time I put on that bathing suit, I'd remember my mother's reaction, and get anxious all over again. All of those feelings got stirred into an emotional knot in my stomach that festered internally over time. *Just stuff it all down and it will go away. Won't it?*

I thought I did a good thing but it made her mad. This was how it started.

Was it wrong for me to try and fix the suit?

Why did it rip apart in the first place?

Was my butt too big?

CHAPTER 1
PLANTING THE SEED

"You're fat!" Sly said with great disdain, *and* in front of all my friends.

It. Was. Mortifying.

And with her proclamation, as per her usual habit, she turned around and exited the room.

You could have heard a pin drop. My friends were very quiet. The expressions on their faces said it all. They were embarrassed for me, uncomfortable, and not sure what to say or do. Their thoughts might have run something like, *Why would her mother say that? Now what do we say to Michele?*

Quite frankly, we were all at a loss for words, because Sly's comment was so unexpected. And it was the *way* she said it – with the intent of being deliberately mean and hurtful. I felt like I had been punched in the gut. I wanted to disappear. Would the ground please open and swallow me up immediately? Her words made me want to cry, always. Crying might get the pain out, but I could never do it in front of her because that would make things worse. She would get angry. I could absolutely *not* cry today, because my tears would embarrass my friends even further. Over time, I would stop crying altogether, because it was seen as a sign of weakness in my family.

My friends and I were all on the parochial basketball team. The year was 1979, and we were all 14 years old. Although boys were starting to become important, we still took our basketball very seriously. We were focused on our practices, our drills, and our games. We were a close group of friends and teammates.

Each school year in order to play on the team, we had to get a physical from the school nurse. Our physical had taken place that very afternoon. At age 14, we were very aware of our developing (or in some of the girls, already developed) bodies, and were naturally curious about each other's height and weight. We weren't competitive about it at all (that would come later in high school). There was no body shunning back then. No vast universe of social media. Only print magazines that showed the super skinny models. Fashionable body types in the year 1979 fell somewhere in between the Twiggy models of the 1960s and the Cindy Crawford supermodels of the 1980s. Before the Kate Moss proclamation of, "Nothing tastes as good as skinny feels." Still, the top models of the late 1970s (i.e. Cheryl Tiegs, Christie Brinkley, Jerry Hall) were thin. A popular TV show was the original *Charlie's Angels* – Kate Jackson, Farah Fawcett, Jaqueline Smith. All three, particularly Kate Jackson, looked dangerously thin. The pressure for women celebrities to be thin continued into the new millennium, courtesy of shows such as *Ally McBeal* with wafer thin Calista Flockhart.

Today, all of this celebrity saturation and more is readily available on social media. No wonder females, and human beings in general, are overexposed to the idea of physical perfection, which is not only impossible, but entirely subjective.

The nurse gave me a paper with my numbers from the physical to take home. It said I was 5'8" tall and weighed 142 lbs. According to kidshealth.org, the BMI (Body Mass Index) calculator put my 14-year-old self at a BMI of 21.6. A BMI of 21.6 is considered a healthy number within normal range. The jaw dropping irony here is that 142 lbs. for a 5'8" tall female of any age is not fat. However, the truth of the matter is that Sly was not capable of seeing her gaffe for what it was - an amazingly cruel thing to say to her daughter in front of her friends. This was just one of countless insensitivities my mother displayed throughout her life. She had no filter. No consideration given to the consequences of her comments, particularly with her children.

As an educated person, I'd like to think my level of intelligence could help me figure this one out. But for the life of me, in the past forty years I cannot think of any logical reason why a mother would say such a thing to her 14-year-old daughter. Bonus points for saying it in front of the girlfriends. What kind of parent does that?

My personal considerations:

- Did she really think I was fat when clearly, I wasn't?
- Was she irritated that I was talking about myself and getting attention from my friends, so she wanted to take me down a notch?
- Was she jealous I was having fun with my friends?
- Was she envious I had my whole life ahead of me, while she was a 36-year-old who felt she didn't have a life?
- Was she taking all of her issues out on me so she could feel better about herself?
- Was she ignorant and thought it was okay to call me fat?
- Did her mother call her fat?
- Am I going to do layperson armchair psychoanalysis on my mother through this entire book? This one I can answer with a resounding *no*. There will be no victim whining. At the very least, it will be kept to a minimum

and only to make a point, because whining doesn't solve anything.

Sometimes it's better to replace whining with humor. A little humor at times can be a godsend, especially in the darkest moments of the starvation illness known as Anorexia Nervosa (AN for short). AN is a dark, horrific nightmare of an illness. AN makes dying look like a completely viable option. A blessed escape.

Sly's words and tone crushed me on this one particular day of my 14th year. Her cruel remarks had occurred before this day, and would repeat countless times after it. Always the cutting remark, a roll of the eyes, an exasperated sigh, a scornful look, a quick exit, or perhaps all of the above. It *hurt*. It hurt bad. I didn't know how to process the pain. I didn't know how to make it go away. I tried to be tough and not let it bother me, at least outwardly. I let the anxiety build, not knowing Anorexia was coming to get me. Soon.

There was something about this incident, however, that really affected me above all the other times. Not to sound too melodramatic, but something inside me died that day. What died? The expectation of a mother that cares for, supports, and above all, loves her daughter unconditionally. It wasn't going to be like that for me. I had to begin to learn how to accept that I wasn't going to get what I needed from her, ever.

Obviously, I was still growing and developing in mind and body. At fourteen, I still thought it was me provoking these kinds of remarks. I was coming up short in some way in meeting her expectations. The classic, *"I'm not good enough"* soundtrack played in my brain constantly. Self-doubt grew steadily and consistently, unfortunately. Not to mention the familiar anxiety since I didn't know when the next insult would be thrown at me. I thought the household in which I grew up in was normal. I figured all parents berated their kids constantly. I didn't know otherwise, so I must be the problem.

Four decades later, I know it wasn't me; it was her. She simply couldn't be the mom I wanted and needed. It took me forty plus years and the death of my parents to believe and appreciate I was not the problem. Again, my story is not a victim's tale. It's a healing saga. I'd honestly like those who are struggling with Anorexia to get to your epiphany quicker than I did. The less time you spend in Anorexia hell, the better. In my adult life, I quizzed my dad Marty about Sly's cruelty. Was she truly ignorant? Marty was uncomfortable talking about it. And the question often came up about whether she wanted children in the first place. But I'm getting ahead of myself.

As a child, I had never given much thought to my height and weight. I also didn't give much thought to food beyond, *I'm hungry, so I'll eat something.* Food was a means to an end. It was fun. I looked forward to mealtime, and I was a hearty eater. Food gave me energy to do all the things I loved to do like playing basketball, soccer, walking back and forth to school every day, and hanging out with my friends. Not to mention studying hard and getting good grades. My brothers and I were straight A students, every year. We would bring our report cards home every quarter, which earned us a special treat. Our local McDonald's rewarded a straight A report card with a free meal. It was the only time we were allowed to have fast food. I always got a cheeseburger, fries, and an orange drink. It was a big deal. Sly would always put a damper on it. She would either complain about having to drive us there, or, even better, she would criticize the occasional A-. "Why didn't you get an A or an A+," she'd say. It was never about the good stuff; it was always whatever negative she could point out. It would sting, but I would stuff it down, and soldier on.

I remember having plenty of energy for sports and school because I ate three squares a day along with snacks. Snacks were fun too, like a candy bar from the small mom and pop convenience store a couple blocks down the street from school. Everyone went there after school for candy and gum. There was a Twisty Freeze ice cream shop right next door to school. It opened in the spring and would get mobbed by students up until summer break. I usually had a little spending money from either babysitting jobs or helping my older brother with his paper route. If funds were low, I could get a blue freeze pop for five cents, but my favorite was the 15-cent soft serve vanilla cone dipped in the chocolate coating that hardened like a shell over the ice cream. You had to eat the chocolate shell first because the ice cream was melting quickly underneath. I enjoyed my food while I was eating it, but once the meal or snack was over, I promptly forgot about it, and got on with the next fun thing. Like most people do. I get very nostalgic for the time before Anorexia hit, because it was the only time in my life when food was normal for me.

My life as a 14-year-old was extremely active. I loved school and playing sports. I had lots of friends. But, oh how everything was going to change, and soon. Fun was going to go away for a long, long time. So was food.

"You're fat!" she said. And thus, the seeds of Anorexia Nervosa were planted.

CHAPTER 2
BATHROOM QUESTION

"What do you think about moving?" Marty asked. He was standing in the hallway just outside the bathroom and talking to me through the closed bathroom door. It was early summer, 1980, and I was 15 years old. I'd just graduated from eighth grade, thus finishing parochial Catholic grade school. My fellow basketball friends would scatter to various high schools throughout the city. These girls and I went through eight years together, and although I was sad I wouldn't be seeing them in the fall, I was excited about starting high school. Many of my friends were going on to Catholic high school, but my family simply couldn't afford it, and that was fine. I never had any trouble making friends, at least not in Erie, PA. I planned to enjoy the last summer with my grade school friends by being out of the house as much as I could. It was what Sly wanted anyway. She didn't want us in the house all day during the summer. She would lock the screen door and tell us to stay gone until dinnertime. No problem, but it wasn't going to be the drill this time. Change was coming. I just didn't know it yet.

"Hold on, Dad, I'll be out of the bathroom in a second." I erroneously thought Marty wanted me to move out of the bathroom so he could use it.

The house we lived in was a single story – 1,056 square feet with three bedrooms and one bathroom. We had lived there since I was a toddler, and it was the only home I knew. Since I was the only girl, I got my own room, while my older brother Mick and younger brother Mark had to share a room. All five of us shared one bathroom. We all learned to get in and out of both the bathroom and the kitchen quickly. Do your business, get what you need, and get out quick. We were a tall family. Marty was 6'5" and Sly was 5'7". I'd eventually get to 5'11". My brothers would reach 6'4" and 6'2", respectively. Five very tall people running multiple schedules in a single-story home of just over 1,000 square feet. Somehow, we made it work.

I opened the bathroom door to see Marty standing there. The expression on his face indicated he was still waiting for an answer to his question.

I said, "I'm all done in the bathroom."

Marty repeated the question, "What do you think about moving?"

I said, "I am moving. Don't you need the bathroom? I'm done here."

Finally, he understood and elaborated. "No, I don't mean moving out of the bathroom so I can use it. I mean all of us moving to Oklahoma."

"Oh," I said. I had no clue what to say. His question came out of left field. I never heard my parents discussing it. No heads up whatsoever. It never dawned on me there was ever the possibility of our moving from Erie, PA. When you live in a small town, your world is, for the most part, familiar and safe. For me, the familiarity and consistency of my environment was a comfort, given the absence of parental nurturing in my life.

Erie, PA, in the 1970s was shrinking in size. Its heyday was the 1960s, when the population peaked at approximately 138,000. Four decades later, it was down to less than 100,000. Erie was part of the rust belt; people were leaving because the manufacturing jobs were gone. By contrast, Tulsa, OK, had a population four times the size of Erie, and since it was an oil town, growth was positive vs. negative. Erie was also a place where people kept a lot of skeletons in the closet. Families swept their bad shit under the rug and kept it there. Women at church would apply their makeup carefully to hide the bruises, but they were still visible. The culture in Erie was more about the *appearance* of normalcy. Dysfunction was dirty laundry. People kept their secrets.

The possibility of moving to Tulsa, OK, caught me completely off guard. It was the last thing I ever expected to hear from Marty. I did learn that it was a job promotion for him, so I didn't want to be difficult about it. It was just so weird that a major life change was an out of the blue bathroom question. Don't families have dinner table conversations for serious shit like this? Not at our house. Not once. My job as the only daughter and the middle child was to go along with everything and not make waves.

I said, "That would be okay, I guess."

Marty said, "Thanks."

And that was it. The big summer of 1980 change I didn't see coming. Obviously, there had to be similar conversations with my two brothers to which I was not privy. A part of me thought, *What does it matter what I think?* If I said, "No, I don't want to go," would it really have mattered, or made any difference?

In hindsight, Marty probably told his boss, "Let me talk it over with my family, and I'll let you know." Marty was a plant manager at the company's branch in Erie. The company made measuring systems for oil. They had a big operation in Oklahoma, and the company headquarters was in Texas. What the new job entailed, we didn't know, other than it was a promotion for Marty. He had to take it to move up in the company.

It became immediately apparent that Sly did not like the idea. At all. She made it clear from the get-go that she did not want to move out to Tulsa. In the end, Marty accepted the job. Neither of my parents had a college degree, so for the company to offer the position to Marty was a big deal. Rejecting the offer would be career suicide. We would move over the summer, and I would start junior high school out there. In Tulsa, school was structured with grades 7-9 as junior high, and grades 10-12 as high school.

Mick would start 11th grade at a different school than us. Mark and I would be the same school, in grades seven and nine, respectively.

Once the move became official I grew increasingly anxious. We were going from a place where I had spent my entire childhood to a completely different environment halfway across the country. I didn't have anyone to talk to about my nervousness. Since I had finished grade school, the basketball camaraderie I had with my friends was also finished. The friend outlet was no longer available to me. In the past, the bond I had with my teammates served as the emotional glue that anchored me when all was not well at home. It gave me what I wasn't getting at home. Take that away and the balance was disrupted. The deficit began. My brothers had their own agendas; you didn't want to hang out with your sister when you were 13 and 17 years old. They were also hanging out with our two uncles, one of whom was teaching them how to smoke pot and liked going after little girls. The other uncle liked boys, any age. Getting away from those bad uncles was their silver lining in this whole abrupt transition. If Mick and Mark had any misgivings about moving, they weren't vocal about it.

At one point I said something to Sly like, "Wow, it's going to be really different out there; I hope I like it." Instead of offering encouragement, or asking me how I felt about it, she simply said, "Well, you were going to start a new school in the fall anyway, so it will be easier for you than your brothers. They don't get to finish like you did. Mick misses grades 11-12 at his high school. Mark misses grades 7-8 at the parochial school. You have it easy."

Wow. Okay...translation...Don't make a big deal of this and don't complain. Suck it up and put on the happy face, even if you're not sure about this. You don't have the right to complain. You're not important enough to have an opinion. Even if you did, no one is going to listen. Do. Not. Make. Waves.

More and more of my thoughts about the big move continued to develop and marinate in my brain as we proceeded with the Erie to Tulsa move throughout the summer of 1980. Those thoughts become like fertilizer. They started feeding the seeds of Anorexia that had been planted just months ago when Sly said, "You're fat."

CHAPTER 3
THE MOVE, PART 1 – TULSA OR BUST

"I'm taking Mitzi to the vet this afternoon," Marty said. Mitzi was a black and white terrier mix and had been our family pet for over eight years. Truly, she was a part of our family; we grew up with her.

I didn't know it at the time, but taking Mitzi to the vet meant Marty was going to have her put to sleep. She was going to be killed. My parents had decided she had to be put down because she was too old to make the trip by car out to Tulsa. My parents gave a vague explanation about how having the dog in the car during the three-day drive wasn't going to work. Stopping to let her out to do her business would be too inconvenient and eat up too much time (but didn't we all have to stop and do our business)? The heat and climate in Tulsa would be too much for seven-year-old Mitzi, who was better suited to the cold Erie weather. My parents thought bringing an animal along would simply be too much to deal with. Marty and Sly were already arguing constantly about this move; our dog added to the stress. It wasn't a decision my brothers and I participated in. It was a practical decision made by Marty and Sly and that was it.

By now, the AN seeds had received sufficient environmental triggers and were fully sprouted in my brain. AN decided it was time to make its opening statement:

AN: "Hey girlie! Let me introduce myself! I'm here now, and I'm going to be your new best friend. I'm brilliant, seductive, and clever. Lucky you. And guess what? Bet you didn't know this is one of my root causes. All of my girls and boys, my beautifully thin anorexics, try to control their bodies by denying food when they can't control what is happening around them. A big transition like this move is going to screw up your family more than it is already. How dare Sly ignore your feelings? I'm gonna get you girlie. You're easy prey."

I remember the summer afternoon clearly. Marty opened the back door saying, "C'mon, Mitzi let's go for a ride." Mitzi knew what the word "ride" meant, and didn't hesitate a second before bounding out the door as Marty held it open. I noticed Mitzi's "dog joy" and the total trust only dogs have for their owners as she followed Marty out the door. That was it. Mitzi was gone. Putting her down was something Marty chose to do solo. None of us kids were invited to come along.

My brothers weren't around when Marty took Mitzi, and I'm not sure where Sly was, but she wasn't home either. Once the back screen door slammed shut, and the car pulled out of the driveway, it was *so* quiet – just a sunny summer afternoon meant for enjoyment and play. But as I sat with the silence and began processing the fact that Mitzi was going to the vet to be killed, I thought, *Wow, this is getting real.* The weird thing is, no one said anything about it, nor did anyone display any emotions over Mitzi's death. We simply proceeded with preparing for the move.

We arrived in Tulsa mid-summer, and stayed in a hotel for three weeks. Nice of Marty's employer to give him plenty of time for us to find a place to live while all expenses at the hotel were covered.

This was exciting for my brothers and me, especially since we could go to the hotel restaurant and order anything we wanted! It was one of the few times growing up, where the three of us took our meals together, which made sense since we didn't know anyone, and hadn't started school yet.

Outside of being holed up in the hotel, my brothers stuck together and I continued my role as the sister they didn't want to hang out with. The exception was when my younger brother Mark and I helped Mick with his paper route back in Erie. We did the paper route primarily so we could earn a bit of spending money for those candy bars after school. We didn't hang out by choice; we needed the money. The paper route was history anyway; we'd have to find other ways of earning money in our new home.

It seemed like back in Erie, we were always hungry, and there was never enough food. We were so active, always doing team sports during the school year, and running around outside all day during the summer. No computers, video games, or social media. My brothers would go with the boys and I'd go with the girls in the neighborhood, and we'd run around all day. There were woods behind our house, so we'd go climb trees, pick berries, make up games, and try not to catch poison ivy.

Having the opportunity to sit down in the hotel restaurant in Tulsa knowing we could order anything on the menu we wanted was a novelty. It felt luxurious. When I opened the menu, I felt like ordering whatever I wanted was wrong somehow. I was so used to hearing 'No' and so used to being criticized by Sly that I didn't feel like I deserved to sit down in a restaurant and order a meal. Eating out (i.e. McDonald's report card day) was a special occasion. My brothers and I always came in without our parents. But it was the hotel restaurant, so it felt safe enough, back in 1980. Pat was the head waitress and often served us when we came in. She took a liking to these three kids who came in everyday and ate heartily. One day as she was delivering breakfast to our table, she said "Waffles will make you *faaaaaaat*." Her Tulsa accent (like everyone out there) was a version of a southern drawl, so when she said the word "fat," the single syllable was *long* and *drawn out: Faaaaaaat*. Talk about a golden opportunity for Anorexia Nervosa! I was 15 years old, hadn't been anywhere or done anything after growing up in small town Erie. Really green, and already well into puberty. And boy was I impressionable. I took Pat's words seriously. Pat unknowingly started a whole new stream of questions in my head having to do with food. She gave AN more ammunition to grow. My first thoughts about this were, *Can certain foods make me fat? Are there foods I should avoid? Is this food bad for me? How can it be bad when it tastes so good and I enjoy it so much?* I was truly puzzled; why did she say that, and what did it mean? We were raised to be seen and not heard, so I didn't question Pat directly. I just ate my waffles, but now it felt different. It was the first time a thin layer of anxiety crept in while I was eating.

AN had begun.

AN: "Yes! The element of negativity around food has been introduced. Behold the universal truth: there are bad foods. Yes! Let us commence with welcoming Michele as a new member of our elite society!"

If the waffles made me fat, then I'd have a harder time transitioning into my new life in Tulsa. At 15 years old, in a new city halfway across the country, I started drawing the comparison between food, the way I looked, and acceptance. The Sly comments started the process and Pat unknowingly reinforced it.

If I chose "bad" food, I might not be accepted. If I chose "good" food, I'd have a better chance of being accepted, because then I wouldn't be fat. Anxiety started ratcheting up as well. *How do I discern between good food and bad food?*

I needed to be accepted, because being unhappy out there in Tulsa would just create an unnecessary burden for my parents to deal with when they already had so much on their proverbial parental plates. I was used to being invisible in the family. It was my role and I played it well. Therefore, I had better learn this new concept of bad foods quickly, so I could avoid them.

To take it even further, if I could learn to discern the difference, would choosing good food and shunning bad food help me gain acceptance from Sly? Did I need to look up what the skinny models had to say? So many questions. I felt like I didn't have anyone I could go to on this topic, which also fed my anxiety.

AN: "Hi there! I'm back again! Girlie, you are doing a great job of meeting my requirements; I couldn't be more pleased. Anxiety, along with depression and perfectionism are key factors I look for. Why do you think it's called Anorexia? I'm going to drown you in anxiety. You just wait and see. You're playing right into my recruitment strategy! I wish I had social media so I could saturate you with thinspiration, but that's coming later. Or how about bonespiration, where I show you how virtuous it is to have your bones protruding from your body? Wait until you see Tumblr – it's my masterpiece! With you, Michele, I cannot wait for social media to be invented. But you know what? You are already catching on. You can do it without social media. You don't need those images of perfect bodies to prove to yourself that you are inadequate. Such an over-achiever, you."

My anxiety level started ratcheting up during this summer of 1980. I suppose it was to be expected, given all the change going on in my life. Dealing with all of it alone was the hardest part.

In addition to anxiety, depression, and perfectionism, studies have shown that over 50% of those with AN have a genetic predisposition to the illness. Whatever touchpoints I had in my genetic blueprint that could evolve into AN lit up with the waffle statement. They were being fed (no pun intended) by environmental triggers. Sly's verbal abuse was taking me down the AN path, and Pat's innocent comment simply provided acceleration. It was the perfect storm; I didn't stand a chance of escaping AN.

I never ordered waffles again during our hotel stay.

CHAPTER 4
THE NEW SCHOOL

On the first day of 9th grade at the new school in Tulsa, OK, I wore a pair of white denim painter's pants, a beige knit top with a hood, and high heeled wedge type lace-up shoes. The beige knit top was V-neck and was tucked into the jeans.

I remember my outfit clearly because I had put a lot of thought into it. In the back of my mind I knew it was totally wrong for the first day in the new school in the new city. But it was the best I could do. I had no clue what to wear for public school, and no one to ask. I had worn a school uniform for eight years, so I never thought about clothes. The look I was going for was artsy bohemian. With the high wedge shoes, I was very tall, well over six feet. I would have preferred flats, but I didn't have any. My height would attract attention, which I didn't want. Any kind of notoriety made me uncomfortable as I was the "invisible person" now. However, as all teenage girls know, if you're not mirroring exactly what the "plastics" wear (aka cool girls, aka mean girls, thank you Tina Fey for the movie explaining all of this!), and you're new, it's going to be almost impossible to fit in.

During homeroom on Day One, I sat in the back row by the window. I wanted to sit in the back so I could scan the classroom and get a sense of who my classmates were. Our teacher, Mrs. Caldwell, was short, middle aged, wore thick glasses and had short curly hair like a helmet. She spoke with the thick accent everyone in Tulsa seemed to have, and which sounded so strange to me. All the words were draaaaawn waaaaaay out. Shortly after the bell rang to start the day, Mrs. Caldwell announced to the class that I was a new student, and asked if I could pleeeeaaaaase come up to her desk to get a paper to fill ooooouuuuut? Her announcement made me cringe. *Damn, damn, damn it to hell.* The last thing I wanted to do was go up to her desk because I didn't want everyone looking at me. I was uncomfortable enough just being there. First day in the new school. *Please don't anyone look at me*, I thought. Everyone looked because this was before cell phones were invented. Student noses were not buried in screens to check out the latest snarky post on social media. Students were snarky live and in-person instead.

As I made my way to the front, I felt all the eyes on me. Sure enough, I heard one of the Plastic-Cool-Mean Girls (PCMs), Kelly, start snickering. She put her hand over her mouth while doing so. Maybe so Mrs. Caldwell couldn't see? I saw. Yes, Kelly was one of the popular ones. I thought, *I'm like an alien from another planet who landed in southern rich girl world.* I could have had a more constructive thought like, *I will flaunt the artsy bohemian thing, and celebrate being different,* but I wasn't confident in myself enough to take that strategy. The PCMs sensed I was uncomfortable and they were not going to cut me any slack. No warm welcome to the new girl. The very thing I was most anxious about was confirmed by those rich girls. I was an oddball and would not be accepted at the new school. No one else in the class said anything. I knew the PCMs wouldn't accept me, but it still stung. I wish I had been strong enough to not give a damn about their judgement, but I wasn't. Their contrived superiority made me feel so inadequate.

The queen of the PCMs was Julie. She had a habit of walking the halls with her chest stuck out because her breasts were large in proportion to her body. *She looks top heavy,* I thought. They looked fake. She liked to parade around naked in the girl's locker room before and after gym class. Her boobs looked too perfect and symmetrical to be real. She must have gotten a boob job. Julie was very proud of them. All the girls wanted boobs like hers, and all the boys wanted to touch them.

Julie also set the standard for the dress code, and her royal court of TCMs followed her exactly. The uniform for 9th grade in 1980 was skin-tight designer jeans. They had to be a dark blue wash. Long, lacquered hair, lip gloss applied just so, and expensive brand name handbags were mandatory or you were nobody. An easy visual reference is the iconic 1980 Brooke Shields ad for Calvin Klein jeans. I didn't have any of those things. You could absolutely tell who had money and who didn't based on their appearance. Money, and the attitude that came with it, was the determination of the popularity hierarchy for 9th grade in Tulsa, OK in 1980.

From the first day, I knew that the clothes, in particular, would not help me adjust, or make friends. It seems superficial now, but as a teenage girl it means everything to have the right clothes. Not only did I not have the right wardrobe, I didn't have enough outfits for public school. Wearing the same thing too often was taboo. Doing laundry was tricky because we only had a washing machine – no dryer. Wet clothes had to be hung up on a clothesline. It could take a week for jeans to air dry, and they would become so stiff that they could stand up on their own, no kidding. I must have said something at home about my clothes, because one Saturday, Marty offered to take me to the store to buy some new jeans. I couldn't believe it. It didn't even matter if they were designer or not – if they were skin tight or not. I was getting a new pair of jeans, plus I was getting to spend some one-on-one time with my dad.

Marty was at the new job most of the time. I'm sure he was putting in extra hours. Since it was a promotion, there was probably a lot to learn, and certainly he must have felt some pressure to be successful at the Tulsa company location.

We went out for a couple of hours on a Saturday afternoon. I don't remember how much the clothes cost, but I remember coming home with one pair of blue jeans and a short-sleeved, button-up bright pink top. They were in a large brown plastic bag. Funny how those details stick. On the way home in the car, I felt really happy. Feeling really happy was rare for me, and it didn't take much. A couple hours of attention from my dad, and I was positively giddy. I had a new outfit to wear to school, and I got to hang out with my dad. Marty seemed happy to be spending time with me too. We come in the door at home. Sly is there and sees us.

Sly: What's in the bag?

Marty: I bought her some jeans for school.

Sly: Why did you do that? We can't afford it! She doesn't *need* new clothes!

We both looked at her and said nothing. There it was, the knife in my gut feeling. Painful. She destroyed the happiness I felt because that was what she did. The painful memory of my great day with my dad and how it was ruined with one comment has never gone away. It was the green bathing suit fiasco all over again.

Come to think of it, if I had a pair of jeans that needed fixing, I would have broken out the needle and thread again. But I couldn't repair what I didn't have. I was either going to wear the same white jeans every day or buy a damn pair of jeans so at least I could alternate between two pairs of pants. I washed both on the weekends and prayed they would air dry before Monday morning. As usual, one negative response from Sly, and all the happy emotions from the day of shopping with Marty were gone. Guess what they were replaced with? You got it. Another painful emotional sucker punch to my gut. I tried hard not to cry.

Fuck!

Marty followed Sly into their bedroom and they proceeded to argue about whatever money he had spent on my new school clothes. I went to the kitchen table and I sat down with my thoughts. Alone. I felt my eyes begin to tear up and berated myself for being too sensitive. I thought about how I could get rid of my ugly emotions. I thought about how much easier it would be if I could just disappear. I would no longer have to be exposed to Sly's verbal abuse.

AN: "I can make you disappear. I will show you exactly how. I am the answer to all of your problems. Stick with me."

On the bright side, at least I had made it through the first day of school. I was getting better at stuffing my feelings down. *Just ignore it. Stuff it down. Suck it up. Don't acknowledge the feelings, and just get through it. Be invisible. It will protect you from emotional pain.*

My feelings really didn't matter, anyway, because I had a pair of blue jeans. A small change, but it really helped me at school. As the year progressed, things started to improve. The PCMs ignored me for the most part. Instead of wallowing in my unpopularity, I sought out others. It took some time, but later in the school year, Janice, Diane, and Ellen had become my new best friends. We all signed up for the basketball team. We weren't the pretty, rich girls. We were the athletes.

Even better news, I was starting to lose weight. Better to be thin in the wrong clothes than fat in the expensive designer jeans.

CHAPTER 5
WHERE'S SLY?

It started out like another ordinary day in Tulsa. We were about eight months into our life out there.

As teenagers, my brothers and I had been independent for years. Latchkey kids circa 1980. We fended quite well for ourselves. We woke up, prepared a quick breakfast of cold cereal, and got ourselves ready for school. We managed our own transportation as well, either walking or catching a lift from Mick. At 17 years old, he had an old Camaro in a lovely shade of burgundy at his disposal. Occasionally he'd give me a ride to school.

Mark and I went to the same junior high. Mick went to the senior high school. We were all into sports big time. Mick was on track to potentially get an athletic scholarship for college. Football in the land of Oklahoma and Texas was like a religion. Both Mick and Mark were quite good. Football programs in both high school and college were high profile. Sports in Erie were a great avenue not only for giving us something fun to do, but also for keeping us out of trouble. Fellow team members were our tribe, our like-minded peers. This helped bridge the gap in many ways as we transitioned from Erie, PA, to Tulsa, OK. Yes, we were different, but playing sports became the common denominator. Of course, all the sports programs we joined were free of charge, so no objections from our parents. We were out of the house, out of their hair, out of trouble. Bonus trifecta.

Back to the regular weekday morning. All of us are getting ready for school; business as usual. Something felt off though. We looked around, and noticed none of Sly's stuff was there. Marty had already left for work. Where was Sly, and why was all of her stuff gone? We contemplated the question briefly, shrugged our shoulders, and headed off to school.

When we got home that evening, Marty had a brief sit down with us. He said, "Mom decided to go back to Erie. She didn't like it here." That was pretty much it. The interesting thing was, none of us was outwardly upset or emotional about it. Why? Speaking for myself only:

- I learned at an early age not to get emotional about anything.
- Getting upset wouldn't really change the situation.
- Any and all emotions I was experiencing upon hearing this news went the usual route.
- Stuff them away. Don't make waves. Don't cause a problem. Be invisible.

In a way, it was a relief. Sly was obviously not happy in Tulsa, and that made her extremely difficult to live with. She was miserable, complained often, and consequently made our lives miserable too. The constant negativity on Sly's part, and the resulting tensions between Sly and Marty had been going on for months. Very unsustainable. Unfortunately, Sly never even tried to fit in. No effort whatsoever was made on her part, which is sad. In hindsight, she had her mind made up to hate Tulsa before we even got there. She never gave it a chance.

After Marty made his statement, he waited for us to process it. "Did she leave a note or say anything before she left?" we asked. "No." Marty said. Wow, okay.

Here's the kicker. A couple of years later, my paternal grandma (Agatha Mason, my North Star), told me a story. After leaving us in Tulsa, Sly showed up at her doorstep in Erie, suitcase in hand. Sly's original plan was to stay with a friend, and apparently that fell through. Grandma was Plan B.

Can you imagine what went through Grandma's mind when she opened the door and saw Sly standing there? Sly's greeting might have gone something like this: "Hi, I just left your son and grand-kids in Tulsa. I was going to stay with a friend, but it didn't work out. Can you take me in?" If Grandma wasn't the saint she was, she would have said, "Are you fucking kidding me?" and shut the door in Sly's face. However, Grandma did, of course, take her in.

Ironically, there is humor in this story if you knew my grandma and Sly. Their relationship over the previous twenty years had been, at best, cool and cordial. At worst, Sly was flat old cold to Grandma. Grandma was puzzled. She told me, "Your mother is cold. I don't understand why." With three sons, Grandma had always wanted a daughter. A loving daughter-in-law would certainly suffice.

Of course, Sly was broken, period. It was one of the many potential relationships she was simply not capable of either developing or nurturing. "Nurturing" was but one of many emotions absent from Sly's DNA.

But wait, it gets better. Sly forbid Grandma to show us any affection. As grade schoolers in the 1970s, our parents would drop us off at Grandma and Grandpa's (he was still alive then) on the occasional Saturday to spend the night. Marty and Sly would go out and have date night. It was during these weekends at Grandma and

Grandpa's house that I started to get the inkling something wasn't right at home. It was like an itch in my brain I couldn't scratch. It was just so different with my grandparents. Grandma and Grandpa were warm, welcoming and kind. They were overjoyed to see us. I never wanted to leave. When our parents came to pick us up, I would get upset. I couldn't show it, though, because if Sly sensed any reluctance, she'd yell and sometimes a beating awaited at home. She said we were being spoiled by Grandma and Grandpa's affection. Sly told Grandma, "You are not allowed to hug my kids. You are not allowed or tell them you love them."

Seriously. Notice how she said, "My kids" vs. "Your grandchildren." An important distinction because, in the end, we three kids were simply extensions of Sly and Marty. We were not individual people in our own right. And where was Marty's voice in all of this? He didn't interfere when this nonsense happened. He chose to stay silent.

Sure enough, Grandma and Grandpa respected Sly's wishes. However, there is a beautiful ending to this particular childhood episode. Grandma and Grandpa didn't need to hug us, although that would have been wonderful. Affection and love radiated from them in waves. They showed it in their actions. They were clever. If I had to put on the act of looking forward to going home at the end of the weekend, so be it. It was worth it.

CHAPTER 6
THE LETTER

Shortly after Sly left Tulsa, my period stopped. Anxiety? Stress? Who knows?

It was a weird time, to say the least. Marty was completely untethered and out of sorts constantly. Perhaps he didn't believe Sly would carry out her threat of leaving (which apparently only Marty knew about). When she left, he was shaken out of his comfort zone. He certainly couldn't support us kids emotionally as that was not his way. He was very distraught and sort of checked out after she left.

As usual, my brothers and I were on our own. Again, we were relieved. The miserable person who was making us all miserable was gone. Dark cloud lifted.

One day I came home from school. The house was empty. I had an idea. I would write Sly a letter to tell her that my period stopped. Would she know why, and would she have any suggestions on what to do? For some reason, the fact that my period stopped really bothered me. Weight loss wasn't the reason. I was still within normal range, and had only lost a few pounds. I thought telling my mother about my problem would be a way for us to bond. There was no boyfriend in the picture, so no chance of pregnancy.

A quick side note here. During the time right after Sly left, I remember how quiet it was in our house. All the drama from Sly was gone. No more fighting between Marty and Sly, with Sly screaming "I hate it here!" The quiet was a double-edged sword. Why? On the one hand, it was blissful. No more parental drama, tension or negativity. On the other hand, the quiet encouraged me to think more. I went more into my head. Lots of self-talk. More and more around food. The quiet was giving AN more strength.

AN: "Yes. I want you to think more and more about food. Food is the enemy. Avoiding food will make you pure and good. Giving up food will make you skinny. Skinny makes you a better person. The more you think about food, the less you will have to think about those ugly emotions. Sly left because you're not thin enough. Serves you right. Deal with it. Don't be a sensitive pussy."

Back to the letter writing idea. Had the cessation of periods ever happened to her? Was it a hereditary thing, i.e. "normal" for the women in our family? I don't know why I was entertaining even a microscopic shred of expectation that Sly would come through for me. Still, I carried the slight hope she might answer my letter, and give me some advice on what to do. Even something like "Are you pregnant?" might have been good. Any kind of response would be okay, really, because at least she would be showing interest in my issue. She would be acknowledging my existence; otherwise I was invisible. I was learning I shouldn't set myself up for disappointment. I couldn't help it, though. My hope died slowly and hard. Later in my life, there would be women who served the role of a mother figure in my life (Grandma in particular), but at this moment, I had no one else to turn to.

I never got a reply to my letter. It seemed as good a time as any to start a diet and exercise program. I thought if I focused on my nutrition and doing a little bit more exercise on my own, I'd achieve the following goals:

- Stress and anxiety about our whole family situation would improve.
- With better food and more exercise, my health would go from great to outstanding.
- Extra training would better prepare me for next year's basketball season, and I'd be a better player.
- Maybe being healthier would jump start my period.

I decided I would just forget about the period problem. I wasn't pregnant, so I'd turn my attention to something else. To start my fitness program, I would jog about two blocks from our house to the public mailbox on the corner. It was hard. It was always windy in Tulsa, so the first few times I did this little bit of exercise, it felt like resistance training. I hadn't exercised in about a year, not since 8th grade basketball. For those two blocks, I had to do a combination of running and walking at first. I ran to the mailbox, touched it, then bent over to catch my breath, and tried to breathe through the stitch in my side. Then I would turn around and walk the two blocks back to the house. I remember thinking, *Well, it's a start.* It was a start, all right.

The AN foundation was in place. AN was the monster bitch that was alive and already talking to me in my head. The classic signs of the illness were progressing rapidly; I just didn't know it. The emergence of restrictions started as I gradually began to implement my new fitness program. Diet. Exercise. Discipline.

Imagine a bell curve. At the beginning, you're on the upswing. Everything's going great. "I'm on the plan and it's working." If it's a normal diet, it is great. Losing weight, feeling good, taking care of yourself. Thumbs up. However, I don't like to use the word, "diet." It means many things to many people, but to me it means deprivation and a slippery slope to big problems.

You continue to go along on your bell curve. Then the curve peaks, and starts the downward trajectory. The diet is no longer healthy.

Whether the origins of Anorexia are genetic, environmental, a combination of both or something else entirely, everything was beginning to line up. The pattern was beginning.

AN: "Michele, you are a fine recruit for my team! You're anxious, depressed, perfectionistic. No one listens to you. Sly has crushed your self-esteem. Poor you. And now you've started a fitness program. You're going to be an easy one to get. A slam dunk. Hey girlie, I can give you what you seek. Stick with me. I'll get you to thinness. You know thinness equals popularity, acceptance, perfection. Fuck Sly. You can get love, approval and attention from other people if you're thin and beautiful."

The realities of the anorexic profile:

- You're a good girl or boy and want to please.
- Perfectionistic
- Genetic predisposition
- Family dysfunction
- Environmental factors such as Tik Tok, Instagram, Tumblr and countless other media influences

Every day had to be "better" than the day before. Diet. Exercise. Discipline. Five more minutes of exercise. Two less bites of food. *I can do this. If I do this, I win. If not, the day is a fail. I can't fail because I'm failing everywhere else. My mom left. The popular girls don't like me.* This is how the thought patterns emerged and solidified for me.

Again, much of the AN research suggests there is a genetic component to the illness. Perhaps the circuitry in the brain is already pre-wired, and once the pattern starts, all the circuitry lights up. Does the brain drive the pattern, or does the pattern drive the brain? Which came first, the chicken or the egg? Regardless, the behaviors take over, and the nightmare begins.

As I thought more and more about food, I started to do weird things. As an example, one day I decided to make a cake. Ever since I was a little girl, I was a baker, starting with my Easy Bake Oven. All I needed to bake cake was a box of Jiffy cake mix, an egg, and water. The light bulb in the easy bake oven baked the cake. Our pantry in Tulsa, however, was not well stocked for baking. I don't even remember who did the grocery shopping after Sly left. Grocery re-stocking became very haphazard.

I looked in the pantry to see what we had on-hand. I found some oats, cocoa, and sugar. I decided to make a chocolate cake. Why didn't I just go to the store and get a cake mix? No, it would be too much of a bother to get someone to take me. Besides, no one else was home, and I didn't want to wait. Why not try to make use of what we had? I was taught from an early age to be thrifty, so I saw this as a sort of a fun challenge. It would distract me so the quiet and AN wouldn't creep into my thoughts.

After I took the cake out of the oven, and let it cool, it was like a block of cement because it didn't have flour or baking soda - the ingredients that make cake the right texture. It was inedible. Not that I would taste it.

AN: "Oh no, girlie, you're not allowed to have cake. Cake, waffles, or any kind of carbohydrates. What the hell is wrong with you? You already know that those are bad foods, and you're not allowed to eat them. They will make you faaaaaaat."

Since AN told me cake wasn't allowed, I threw it away.

CHAPTER 7

THE MOVE, PART 2 – ERIE OR BUST

In the summer of 1980, we had to move back to Erie.

Why? Because Marty wanted to reconcile with Sly. A quick note here about why I call my parents by their first names. It's not out of disrespect, but rather it enables me to detach myself from painful memories. My parents did not provide the love, support, or encouragement I needed as a child. Instead, there was hyper criticism and physical punishment from both. A frequent threat from Sly was, "Wait until your father gets home." When he did, it was a beating, sometimes just a smack upside the head, or a belt used as a whip. Never enough to cause marks, but enough to hurt both physically and mentally long after the beating was over. The funny thing here is that Sly would scold Marty for hitting me on the head, but any other kind of beating was okay. Imagine being a kid with a 6'5" angry guy coming at you with a belt. Their parenting style was a perverse psychological shock treatment that conditioned me to believe I was inferior in all things when in fact I was an intelligent, creative, attractive child. Those positive things were diminished for a long time, but they weren't destroyed.

My mother never said, "I love you," to me or anyone else. My mother simply wasn't capable of parental love. Later in my life, my dad professed his love for me. To refer to them as Mom and Dad would assume some type of nurturing emotional bond existed between them and me during my childhood years. It did not.

Marty's decision had significant, life changing repercussions for all of us, particularly Mick. As a high school junior, he had been a stand-out on the football team. He was 6'4" and 280 lbs., a force to be reckoned with on the gridiron. His coach had told him that Tulsa University, Oklahoma State, and Arkansas College scouts were interested. His coach wanted to make sure Mick continued to work hard to have the best athletic scholarship opportunities available. Good for the student athlete, getting the full ride, and good for the reputation of the high school and their football recruiting program. Going into his senior year at Tulsa Memorial, Mick would have been the starting left tackle. His senior year team went on to win the state football championship – without Mick.

Mick's teammates and coaches lobbied aggressively on his behalf. Parents of teammates urged Marty to let Mick stay and finish out his high school career. Both coaches and the parents of select teammates said, "He can stay with us." Mick had been offered a promotion at the store where he worked while not at school or football practice. The money from that job would have been sufficient to cover living expenses during his senior year. Everything was lined up in Tulsa to give him the best chance of success after high school graduation.

Marty said no to all of it. Really, Marty? What a hardass. You can't even entertain the idea of giving your kid a shot at a full college scholarship? Most parents would be proud. But Marty was all about going back to Erie, come hell or high water.

Younger brother Mark was coming up through the ranks also, and was already observed as having the skills to be in the 1.6% of college football players (www.nca.org), with a shot to make sports a professional career. He would have been exposed to the same outstanding Oklahoma football programs, both high school and college. Really, success was almost guaranteed for both given they continued to work hard and avoided injury.

Obviously, opportunities in Tulsa were exponentially greater than Erie, PA, for all of us. Tulsa was four times the size of Erie, with an outstanding school system; Erie simply could not provide the same opportunities for advancement. So, in a sense, they were cheated, and that bothered me *a lot*. Again, I stuffed down all those emotions, because no one in my family was able or willing to listen, much less lend sympathy or support. AN *loved* the whole moving back to Erie shit show.

AN: "Oh girlie, you're so pathetic. There you go being all sensitive again. How tiresome and boring. You don't need feelings. You have me! Together we will work to get you thin, and all will be well. Being thin is the most important thing. When you're thin, life is wonderful, and all of your problems go away. It doesn't matter if you're living in Tulsa or Erie. It doesn't matter that going back to Erie is a huge mistake. You and I both know it. You don't have control over where you live. You can control losing weight. That is all you need to focus on. Nothing else matters. Trust me."

Having to move around a lot as a kid wasn't anything new. We'd all heard stories of people that grew up this way. Some thrived on it and became great successes in life, and some tanked and never reached their potential. Everything depended on the individual, right?

But why Marty said no to Mick's great opportunities remained a mystery. The chance for him to get a free ride to an outstanding college was so close. Perhaps Marty felt it was important to keep the

family together. Or he simply didn't realize the possible consequences of moving back. Or he thought Mick could get a scholarship anywhere.

For me, the timing of it all was uncanny; it happened just as I
was reaching my stride in Tulsa. I was starting to really enjoy
school, my new friends, and was having *fun*. The emotional impact
was accumulating for me – I was internalizing all of the repercussions for both my brothers and me. I had no input in the decision,
just like everything else. I continued with my drill to accept, say
nothing and make the best of it. I tried to downplay how upset I
was, but it was a big deal. One day I was happy in Tulsa, and the
next I was looking at boarded up buildings in Erie. Another layer to
my emerging illness began; depression kicked in and ran tandem
with Anorexia.

During my hospitalization, the doctors told me that Anorexia is
the symptom of a bigger problem at home. In my case, much of the
dynamic within the family during the move part two was not good.
In fact, it was fractured. Growing up in a household where affection
and love was neither given nor received was one thing. I had
learned to deal with that. But this new development exacerbated
our particular family dysfunction.

I don't think Marty could see any of this. In his later years, when
I asked him about why he decided to go back to Erie, he said it was
because he didn't think he could be a single parent, and that having
only one parent around wouldn't be good for us. A very traditional
way of thinking, but it didn't ring true to me. It sounded lame. In
1981, all three of us were teenagers. In a few short years, we would
all be out of the house anyway. We had never had both parents
actively engaged in our upbringing. What would it matter now
whether both parents were physically present? Nothing would
change. Even if it did, it was too late in the game.

Marty and Sly came from the parenting school of: "We give you food, clothing, a roof over your head, and school. Be grateful. When you're 18 years old, you're on your own; our work is done." In their minds, that was the definition of good parenting, and represented what we got, no more and no less. As an extension of my parents, my job was to make them shine. My wins made them look good and my failures made them look bad. Plain and simple. Unfortunately, even the wins, like getting all As on my report card, weren't validated by them. They were expected. It was too much pressure to be perfect all the time, yet another reason why it was better to simply be invisible.

I think the real reason Marty decided to go back was that he truly loved Sly; he was willing to sacrifice his career and uproot the kids. Not to mention forgiving her departure and backing out of a job promotion within a year's time.

These exterior events happened so quickly that, even if I had known how to process them, I would have needed more time. These circumstances helped set the stage perfectly for AN to manifest fully. It was a subtle, continuous, cumulative shift in my thinking. It's not like I woke up one morning and said, "I'm not eating anymore." It was far more complex as the medical community has come to realize and begun to document over the last four decades. Of course, internalization of all my emotions didn't help either. But, I was a 15-year-old girl whose mother had abandoned me. I wasn't good enough.

At least the jog to the mailbox was getting easier.

CHAPTER 8
AND SO IT BEGINS...

Upon arrival back in Erie, I was enrolled at Academy, a public school for grades nine through twelve. After ninth grade, I would switch over to Tech Memorial, another public school, for grades ten through twelve. Both Academy and Tech were "burnout schools." Definition of a burnout school: the majority of the student body was not much interested in getting an education. It was about partying and getting high.

Ninth grade was fairly uneventful. I didn't like Academy. The quality of the education, or lack thereof, truly sucked. However, by now, I had gotten used to being the new girl, and all the accompanying increased scrutiny. The standards for peer acceptance in Erie were much lower than in Tulsa. I didn't need the designer jeans or shiny lip gloss, because very few people in Erie had money. I met my friend Jennifer while at Academy. We would hang out on the weekends. We went camping and did a lot of baking. I stayed over at her house several times. Her parents were very kind to me. I felt a strong sense of family at her home, amongst Jennifer, her older sister, and her parents. I craved a warm, nurturing environment, and would take it anywhere I could find it. Jennifer's family lived in an affluent neighborhood in town, but never put on airs. Nor did they carry the sense of entitlement often associated with the wealthy demographic. They were just very kind, warm human beings. Observing all of this continued to solidify my growing conviction that something was seriously awry in my family. The more comparisons I had, the more I could see that the way my parents behaved toward me was not normal.

However, even though this was a bright aspect to the year, AN was getting stronger and was occupying more of my thoughts. I had no idea that this illness was taking over, nor how serious it would become. I had no idea of the road I was going down, and that if I didn't stop going down that road, it would be fatal. The vicious, unrelenting aspects of AN *love* ignorance. Underestimating AN is a big, big mistake.

One of the AN symptoms was obsessive compulsive disorder (OCD). It is more prevalent in some cases than others. For me, it was huge. It strengthened upon repetition like the grooves on a vinyl record. It gained serious momentum in my first year at Tech. I was a 15-year-old high school sophomore – prime time for Anorexia. As AN victims know, it becomes war. You lose. AN wins. At the beginning anyway. The seductiveness is irresistible.

My daily food intake gradually decreased. It consisted of an apple for breakfast and a half of a peanut butter sandwich for lunch. I didn't have to worry about dinner during the week because everyone in the family was doing their own thing. If we happened to sit down to dinner on the weekend, I ate as little as I could get away with. An evening snack before bed would be one to one-and-a-half cups of granola cereal. Yes, I measured it out precisely. The amount had to be either the same or less than the day before. More would be a fail; AN would not allow failure. If I ate dinner, I could not have the cereal later, because AN said that would be too much.

It had to be one or the other. Cereal or dinner, not both. Every day, AN got stronger in my brain. Eventually, it would not even occur to me to defy AN even when I was so hungry I felt like I was going to pass out.

This meager amount of food was supposed to sustain me through a day of school, which included basketball practice. I had learned to restrict food intake in Tulsa the previous year and was proud of my discipline. Lo and behold, it was working, and I continued to lose weight rapidly.

AN: "See, what did I tell you? Sly said you were fat. She might like you better if you slimmed down, you know. Why worry about shit you can't control? Just stop eating, that's all you have to do. Easy."

Kids at school didn't say anything at first. As my sophomore year progressed, however, the stares grew more frequent. My friends in art class were exceptional; they tried to protect me from nasty comments, although one day a student walked by me in the hallway, and I heard him call me a Cambodian refugee. He laughed as he said it. What an ignorant asshole.

My clothes were getting baggier. One day I had on a pair of khaki denim overalls. I had walked into the TV room where Sly was watching a show. I walked past her, and she grabbed the fabric on the seat of the pants. She always had long, pointy nails, real ones, not fake. My rear end had shrunk and didn't fill in the pants. So, she kept pushing in with her nails until she pinched my ass. I could feel her talons trying to grab my skin, and when she got hold, it really *hurt*. She said, "You're too skinny, what's wrong with you?"

What? Here we go again. What the fuck. First, I'm too fat, now I'm too skinny? Make up your mind, Sly! No matter what weight I was, there would be a snarky comment from Sly. It became more and more important to take control of my life by taking control of my food. If I could get to the so-called society's idea of thinness, maybe things would change at home – maybe something more than just shelter, food and clothes.

AN: "Sly is just jealous because you've lost weight and you look better now. I'm not the symptom of a bigger problem. I'm giving you the solution. I'm delivering you from all of your problems, including Sly. If you don't appreciate that, then you're an ungrateful bitch. This is all on you. All you have to do is focus on getting skinnier. Thinness trumps all."

CHAPTER 9
BASKETBALL

"Wow, you're really tall, do you play basketball?" I've heard that question countless times throughout my life, usually when I was a barhopping twentysomething and a guy wanted to start a conversation.

I was always one of the tallest, if not the tallest girl in my class. It seemed like a no brainer to try out for the basketball team. I made the team and played every year through high school. I wasn't a standout player, but it was really fun, and isn't that what grade school sports should be? Basketball was a big part of my life from fourth to eleventh grade.

You have to find your tribe in school. For me it was my teammates. Playing sports kept me busy and out of trouble. I didn't have time to fall in with the wrong crowd. Basketball taught me the importance of healthy competition, discipline, hard work, focus, and determination. The lessons have served me well over the years. The teams I played on were never winning teams. That wasn't the point, as far as I was concerned. It was being part of the tribe and it was fun. Fitting in somewhere is so important when you're a teenager trying to find out what you're all about as a human being.

All of the girls on the team worked really hard. One day at practice, our forward, Sue, announced to Cindy, our assistant coach, that she had lost ten pounds. Cindy said, "Great!" As I overheard this conversation, I thought, *Okay, in the world of basketball, losing weight is good, so gaining weight is bad.* I filed the information away for future reference. This is very black and white thinking, true, but at 14 years old I desperately wanted approval and constantly looked for ways to get it. If I couldn't get it from my mother, then I'd take it from somebody. Anybody.

Our coach always said games could be won or lost on free throws, so I worked extra hard on those. When you got fouled by a player on the other team, you could stand at the free throw line and shoot without interference. Free throws ended up being my biggest contribution to the team. I didn't score a lot of points as a forward, but I made most of my free throws. The Knights of Columbus had a free throw competition. Coach said I should do it, so I did. Whoever made the most out of 25 free throws would move ahead in their age bracket. I moved through the city, district, and regional contests. I made it to the final state contest and won by making 23 out of 25 free throws.

In grade school, practice was every day, Monday through Friday. My weekdays went like this:

- Rise, put on the parochial uniform, and eat a bowl of cereal for breakfast.
- Walk to school. Add a few extra minutes during the winter to pile on the snow gear before heading out.
- School until 3:30pm.
- Walk home, do homework, have a snack.
- Walk back to school for basketball practice, 6-8pm.

- Walk home at 8pm. Eat whatever was left on the stove and go to bed.

Since basketball was always in the winter when it got dark around 5:00 pm, I was always walking by myself in the dark, but was never really afraid. It wasn't far and the route was through safe neighborhoods with a lot of street lights.

One winter night I came home, and there was a saucepan on the stove with three hard boiled eggs. I sat at the kitchen table, in the dark, alone, eating those eggs. I thought about my teammate Kim. She was one year ahead of me in school and was another starting forward on the team. Her mother had arrived to pick her up after practice. As I was putting my coat and boots on for the walk home, I heard her say to her mother, "I want a cheeseburger and fries from McDonald's." Kim was enjoying a cheeseburger and fries while I was eating hard boiled eggs. And she didn't have to walk home in the cold and dark every night.

I didn't feel any emotion in comparing my dinner to Kim's. It was more like curiosity and surprise. Curiosity around what would it feel like to have my mother pick me up from practice and take me to dinner. Surprise that some kids went to McDonald's on a regular weeknight (without a report card), and the parents paid for the meal. When I recalled the conversation between Kim and her mother, it seemed so routine. It sounded like something they did all the time. I knew that would never happen for me because my mother was different. Maybe those three hard boiled eggs were all I deserved. Maybe I didn't deserve a meal at Mickey D's unless I had the straight A report card and got the food for free.

My pre-adolescent brain gradually formed the idea that something in my family might not be normal. The way my mother treated me might be different from how other mothers were with their daughters, and not in a good way. It was a fleeting thought I hid away in my subconscious. We didn't do feelings in my family, so even if I had been envious of my friend, or vocalized the "Sly, why don't you act more like Kim's mom?" question, it wouldn't have gained any traction at home. In fact, it probably would have resulted in physical discipline, because I would be sassing my mother. Sly would wash my mouth out with soap, using the pink dish detergent that made me gag. Or she would grab my hair and pull some of it out of my head. Clumps of my hair would be in her fist, with her long sharp nails wrapped around it, while she screamed at me. Yes, something here was off. A normal mother wouldn't pull her girl's hair out, would she?

Basketball in my junior year of high school was a major turning point. Why? AN was creeping in. It was getting exponentially more difficult to get through practice. A game that used to be fun wasn't fun anymore because I wasn't fueling my body and had zero energy. I was getting weaker. Fast.

AN: "You don't need fuel to play basketball. Even eating three hard boiled eggs is too much. You can get by with less. I will show you how. This is part of the discipline you've always applied to sports; we're just taking it up a notch. You will be a lean, spectacular ballplayer."

This is how AN works on the psyche. AN is an evil monster bitch. A large spider spinning a big sticky web. And very seductive. It knows exactly what to say and when. And then once you're in the sticky web, there's no turning back.

One day at practice, I was on the court, practicing my dribbling, doing lay-ups, and warming up. Coach came up to me, put his hand on my back, and said, "Michele, you need to eat something." He went back to the sidelines and started talking with the assistant coach. They were both looking at me.

He could certainly see my decline in body mass and strength – enough to say something. He was compassionate about it. I said something like, "Yeah, okay." Inside I was embarrassed. The food deprivation was something I was doing to better myself. I felt like I was doing it in a vacuum, and didn't expect anyone to notice or say anything. It felt really good to have control over something. Upholding the AN eating rituals was the primary thing. Losing weight as a result was secondary.

It also felt weird because I wasn't used to the attention. Obviously, coach was concerned. He probably didn't want me to pass out during a game, or have health issues under his watch. I had turned into a potential liability for the team. For him to take me aside and say something was an indicator of how frail I looked. When AN forced me to quit the team, I never went back.

Here's another example. In November of 1980, while I was doing school and basketball, I decided to take on a seasonal job at Hickory Farms at the big mall in town. Pre-internet, everyone flocked to the mall to shop for Christmas. Founded in 1951, Hickory Farms sold sausage and cheese gift packages, which were hugely popular during the holidays. I thought it would be a good way to earn some spending money, and it was only for about four to six weeks during the holiday season. My job was giving out samples to the shoppers and encouraging them to buy gift packs. At this point, I was 5'11" and about 125 lbs., and they hired me. I looked thin, but not in the danger zone yet.

There was a mandatory training prior to our first day on the floor. I arrived at the store and went to the back with about six other seasonal workers. The manager was a pleasant 25-ish year old lady with straight, dark hair halfway down her back. She had the Hickory Farms apron on, and had some extra padding around her middle. Not much, maybe twenty pounds. She was going to teach us the proper way to give out samples. She had one of the summer sausages in one hand and a paring knife in the other. She demonstrated how to cut off the right sample portion and offer it to the customer without touching it. Then we all had to practice the technique with her via role play. We were the samplers, and she was the customer. We all did a turn, and so she ended up eating several sample slices of the summer sausage. That was the extent of our training.

I watched in fascination as our trainer ate bite after bite. Sausage had become foreign to me. I couldn't remember the last time I had a piece of meat. It wasn't allowed under AN's rules.

During this seasonal work, I made about $300. However, people started occasionally giving me funny looks. One customer even said, "You should eat some of that sausage you're sampling," kind of in a joking way. It was becoming noticeable no matter how many layers of clothes I put on. Whenever I went into work thereafter, instead of having fun with the job, and enjoying the holiday season, I began to worry if someone would say something.

That is what happens with AN. It contaminates the things you love. Activities become so difficult when you're starving that they're not fun anymore. You think about food all day long. The hunger and fatigue never ends, and gets worse as the day goes on. You think about when you'll be allowed to eat again, and no matter the portion size, it won't be enough. It is triumphant misery. It is the ultimate oxymoron.

AN: "Do this job if you want. In fact, with school, basketball, and this job, the weight will fall off of you. Top that off with the restricted eating. Exactly what we want. But Hickory Farms beef sausage? Cheese? Are you fucking kidding? If any of those stupid customers comment on how you look, it's because they are jealous. Don't you even think about eating that stuff. No samples for you, girlie. I will not allow it, and I own you now."

CHAPTER 10
TEA AND MORE TEA

My food intake got more and more ritualistic during the second half of 1980.

The daily intake of an apple, half a sandwich and a cup of granola was woefully inadequate for my height, age, and activity level. It was simply unsustainable, yet I ate this way from the summer of 1980 until early 1981, a total of approximately eight months.

For the meager half sandwich lunch, the peanut butter had to be spread evenly to the ends of the bread. The less used to accomplish this the better. I made it into a game. The goal was to cover the bread to the edges with the least amount of peanut butter possible. Each day the layer either stayed the same or became microscopically thinner. If I used less peanut butter than the day before, it was a win. To use more than yesterday was a fail and meant I was a weak pussy. It had to be the same amount or less, and my thoughts had to validate it. This was where the ambiguity lay. It might not even have been my thoughts; it might have been AN dictating to my brain what was acceptable. The line between my voice and the voice of

AN was becoming blurred. Whenever my thoughts veered to how weird and crazy this was getting, AN simply overrode them. It was never an option to defy AN.

The OCD behaviors started to become more pronounced. Every day, the preparation of the half sandwich had to be done exactly the same way. The false sense of structure, order, and control continued to build. It became my lifeline. What would I do without it? It would feel like a free fall. On the other hand, who wants to spend an hour of their life everyday counting out granola pieces? Eventually I would starve to death, and end up at the pearly gates in heaven trying to explain what the fuck happened. The Pearly Gatekeeper Angel would ask, "Michele, what did you do with your short life?"' And I would say, "Not much. I spent a ridiculous amount of time in 1980 and 1981 scrutinizing bags of granola in my bedroom. Angel, why did I get AN? Can you send me back so I can try again?"

It took me a whole hour to eat the half sandwich at lunch in the school cafeteria. I'd perfected the art of making it look like I was eating but I was not. In the 10th grade, I took half a day of "shop," (i.e. vocational studies), to prepare for life after high school should I choose to skip college, or if I couldn't afford it. I was to be trained in a vocation, so I could make a living. I chose commercial art, which lasted all morning. I was naïve. I thought I could pursue art because I had always loved drawing and painting – it didn't matter if I went to college. After lunch, academic studies were in the afternoon. My commercial art friends ate lunch with me. They were worried, but didn't say anything. Back in 1980, no one really talked about eating disorders. Pre-social media, we knew, in a vague way, what eating disorders were. But they didn't happen to anyone we knew, especially in uptight, Catholic, conservative Erie, PA. As a result, no one really knew what to do or say.

In the evening, it was tea and more tea. I put on my pajamas and went to the kitchen to heat up the tea kettle. I grabbed a mug, put the teabag in, and poured in the boiling water. I drank it black for zero calories. From the kitchen to my bedroom, I had to go up about six steps, since we lived in a split-level plan house. As I got weaker from the weight loss, those stairs became harder to manage. I was so afraid I would spill my tea. When I got to my bedroom, I would feel out of breath and dizzy. It was agony getting up those stairs because I was so weak. I drank cup after cup of hot tea before bed because I was so hungry, and it helped to fill up my empty stomach. To go with the tea, I kept the bag of granola in a drawer in the night stand by my bed. I carefully portioned out granola pieces to eat for my meager, so-called evening meal. This was my favorite ritual of the day. I got to reward myself for being good all day. I carefully selected the granola pieces I wanted to eat from the bag. It took me a long time to choose which granola pieces and how many. In a new bag of granola, there were big clumps, along with the rest of the oats and dried tasteless raisins. The big clumps were the prized pieces, so I chose them carefully, but only allowed myself one big clump per meal. I always had just the oats and honey flavored granola with a few token raisins because extra ingredients would add too many calories. The granola I ate was a generic brand and came in a plastic bag about the size of a small pillowcase. I always got the same kind, and it took forever to finish a bag. The longer I could make the bag last, the better. I followed this drill every night. If I didn't follow the sequence in exactly the same way, I got anxious. Worse yet, if something happened to deviate from this process, I'd get angry. For example, if I was slowly making my way up the stairs with my hot tea, and one of my brothers saw me. I didn't want anyone to see me; I didn't want to have to talk to anyone. I wanted to go into my bedroom, close the door, and do my ritual. I got my skeletal self through the ordeal of another day, and I wanted to do my ritual. I *needed* to do my ritual.

OCD made me scrutinize that damn cereal forever. I'd take a clump out of the bag, put it in a cup, then put a bit more in to fill up the cup to about three quarters full. I'd look at it and say, "No that's too much," or "No, that piece is too big, or too small." I put pieces back in the bag and took them out again, back and forth, countless times. OCD autopilot. When I finally decided the amount and composition was just right, I could have it. I would take a small piece of granola and a sip of tea at the same time. I let the hot tea soften the hard oats, then swallowed. Of course, I made it last as long as I possibly could. If it took 45 minutes to prepare; it took at least an hour or two to eat it. With pajamas, a bathrobe, and three blankets covering me, I sipped my hot tea and finally got warm after freezing all damn day. This was the best part of my day, hands down, because I could hide in my bed and be invisible.

Doesn't this sound totally and completely crazy to you? You're absolutely right. The whole process was excruciating. As I was doing the OCD thing night after night, it felt like I was watching myself in a movie. A part of me thought, *This is ridiculous; this is insane. This is not good.* I knew it was crazy as I was doing it. I. Could. Not. Stop.

Again, the rituals coupled with OCD (and let's not forget the depression, anxiety, and perfectionism) were the things that gave me my power and control. They became the thing. The weight loss became the by-product of the thing. I never looked at my body. I knew my clothes were getting looser, but I just ignored it.

Most of the time, when I finished the cereal and tea, I felt full for the first and only time of the day. I only let myself feel full at night right before bed, because I had become more and more uncomfortable with feeling full, so going to sleep right after eating was the solution. Feeling full was a fail. It meant I couldn't control my eating.

Some nights I was still very hungry after I ate what I had

portioned out. Did I ever go back and get more? Absolutely not. I would shut off my bedside light and lie in the darkness, thinking about my hunger before falling asleep. A little bit of hunger was a good thing. It meant I had discipline. I could stop eating before I ate too much and got fat. I was terrified of losing control with my eating. I began to feel that the whole situation was becoming hopeless. Despair and exhaustion crept in. I distinctly remember thinking, *I'm still so hungry, and I won't get to eat again until lunch tomorrow. I can't do this all over again; it's impossible for me to do one more day of this nightmare.*

Death started to look attractive – when not waking up the next morning felt like a better choice. But there was no choice. The next day dawned and Anorexia did it to me again, over and over. I was completely trapped and it was beyond excruciating. There are no words that can capture anorexic hell. Depression increased and layered onto the OCD. Anorexia fed on my psyche while I fed on nothing.

This extreme pattern repeated itself every day through the latter half of 1980 and into the beginning of 1981. This was how I lost 30% of my body weight over eight months. Consider, too, that at 5'11" and about 150 lbs. when this all started, I wasn't fat to begin with.

This is how AN works. AN sufferers don't stand a snowball's chance in hell of stopping it on their own. Once I passed the point of no return with this horrific illness, it became impossible to break out of it without outside help. I was powerless to stop, truly. The rituals became deeply ingrained in my psyche.

It is so, so important for friends and family to step in lovingly, and say something, anything – because AN is a dangerous monster bitch. Outside support is crucial to break the grip of AN.

AN: "Yes, I know I'm a dangerous monster bitch. I thrive on it. Don't even try telling the people that someone should step in and help my recruits. No one can outsmart me."

CHAPTER 11
THE DOCTOR VISIT

"I can't believe I have to take you to the doctor for this," Sly said scornfully. The tone of her voice was like an emotional punch in my gut. I hated it when she yelled at me. I just wanted to disappear.

It was March 1981. I had just turned 16 years old in February.

AN was having a complete *field day* with me. The bitch was winning.

AN: "I'm winning! I know I'm winning! See how pissed off you've made your mother? Well done! And did you catch how it's all about her? You are creating a problem for her because she has to take you to the doctor. No, you're not creating a problem, you are the problem, and always have been."

It was late afternoon, around 4:00 pm. I had just come home from school. Sly was the only one home. March in Erie is cold, dark and dreary. It matched my mood perfectly at that point. Sly grabbed the car keys, and I followed her out the door. I didn't want to go to the doctor. I was freezing, exhausted, and anxious. Most of all, I didn't want to be in the car listening to her bitching at me. Defying Sly was not an option, so I got into the front passenger seat. I huddled into myself for warmth. Even with the heat on in the car, I was still freezing. Over the past eight months, as my body weight disappeared, I got colder and colder. By March I was never warm, no matter how many layers of clothes I piled on to hide my skeletal body. As Sly was driving to the doctor, she continued to go off on her ranting and complaining. Taking me to the doctor was such an inconvenience for her. All I could think of was that Marty must have told her to take me, so she was angry she had to do it instead of him.

I unconsciously started to shift away from her in the passenger seat. I leaned as close as I could to the door and window on my side of the car, even though the surface was very cold. I tried to make myself very small. Her verbal avalanche made me want to disappear entirely; I would rather have been anywhere else than in the car with her. As cold as I was, it was better to lean on the frosty window than be near her.

It was confusing. I knew I was in trouble. I knew my condition had turned serious, but I didn't how to stop it. Remember the seed had been planted when I was 14. Although I didn't start losing weight until the following year, Anorexia's powerful thought processes had started to kick in. Even worse, having just turned 16 in February, my body was still developing, yet it was in starvation mode.

I didn't understand why Sly wasn't showing even a miniscule amount of concern over what was going on as we were riding along. Couldn't she see that I was distressed and scared out of my mind? I didn't say anything. There was no point. But surely my body language said what I could not.

As I was huddled in the small ball, trying to disappear, there was a question. *Why is she making me feel bad about myself? I haven't done anything wrong. She told me I was fat two years ago. I've slimmed down. I did what she wanted. Why can't she say something good about me for a change?* It was always about me causing problems for her, and being more trouble than I was worth. Constant criticism whittled away at my confidence and self-esteem, until there was nothing left.

We arrived at the office of our family doctor. Dr. D had been our family doctor ever since I could remember. Fortunately, my brothers and I were very healthy and rarely had to see a doctor for anything. The only other time I saw Dr. D in recent years was October 1980 because I had stopped having my period again, no doubt due to weight loss. All the usual tests were done including a white/red blood cell count, cholesterol, and triglyceride levels. All were normal. My weight in October 1980 was 127 lbs. Therefore, nothing further was done. Prior to October, I hadn't been to the doctor since 1974 when I was seven years old.

On this day in March 1981, a physical exam was done. Notes from the exam:

- General: She is pale. She is a very cachectic looking (i.e. a physical wasting with loss of weight and muscle mass) white female.
- Vital Signs: Her weight is 101. Her heart rate is around 62.
- Eyes: Her eyes are sullen and sunken.
- Ears: TMs (tympanic membranes) are clear.
- Throat: No inflammation.
- Neck: There are no carotid bruits (a vascular sound checked for that may lead to an arterial pathology leading to a stroke) and no thyroid bruits (a continuous sound that is heard over a thyroid mass).
- Lungs: Sound clear.

- Heart: No murmurs, rubs or gallops. The rate was stated at around 60 (normal range is 60-100 beats per minute, resting).

We were in the examining room. I was standing between the doctor and Sly. Dr. D asked me to take my shirt off. He stood about six feet behind me. I was facing Sly, who was sitting in one of the spare chairs against the wall. Once I had my shirt removed, Dr. D asked me to raise my arms up to shoulder height and hold them straight, forming a T. He was silent for about a minute. Then he quietly said to Sly, "She needs to go to the hospital. Now."

(As a side note, Dr. D, as of this writing, is still practicing medicine some forty years later. Remarkable. He declined to be interviewed for this book, and I totally respect his decision and privacy. Regardless, with his quiet statement, he saved a life. Mine.)

Upon hearing his instruction to Sly, AN started screaming:

AN: "You can't go to the hospital. You know we have to go home to do the nightly tea and granola thing. And you have to make the cereal amount a few grains less than last night. You need a new goal – let's get below 100 lbs. You can't be 101. We need to get your weight from triple digits to double digits. How are you going to do tea and granola at the hospital? They won't let you. Oh, no, we can't have this. It is completely unacceptable. You are a world-class loser for letting this happen. However, this doesn't end the game. Oh no. We will simply have to be extra clever and sneaky. It will be fun. I will show you more food tricks. Do you think you're the first of my recruits to end up in the hospital?"

At this point, despite feeling like I was going to collapse most of the time, I didn't care anymore. I was tired mentally and physically.

With both Sly and AN beating up on me, there was a cumulative effect that had more than taken its toll.

And, at 5'11" and 101 lbs., I had entered the danger zone. My heart felt like it had to work harder to pump blood through my blood and keep all the systems functioning. It was harder to breathe. My joints and muscles felt sore. I had that weird baby fine lanugo hair on my arms, which is the body's way of trying to warm itself. My body felt like it was starting to shut down. Truth be told, I was depressed, I didn't care and all I wanted to do was sleep. I wanted all of it to go away. I wanted to check out.

For once, Sly didn't say anything. Dr. D's statement was enough to convey the seriousness of the situation. We left his office, went home, and I packed a bag. We proceeded to the hospital. I was admitted on the evening of March 24, 1981.

Dr. D's Notes on 3/24/81:

Impression:

- Weight loss, etiology is to be determined, rule out Anorexia Nervosa, rule out some underlying endocrine problem.
- Amenorrhea, probably secondary to the above.
- Previous history of mild bradycardia.

Plan:

Admit her and do a complete underlying workup and determine problems in the future.

That night was the first night I had ever spent in the hospital. It felt like the bottom had dropped out of my world. I no longer had control, yet I was too worn out to keep going with the control.

Now it got real. The work began. I was too weak. *I can't do it.* I was in despair.

CHAPTER 12
THE HOSPITAL, PART 1 – MEDICAL UNIT

Upon admittance to the hospital on March 24, 1981, my vital signs were:

- Height: 5′11″
- Weight: 101 lbs.
- Heart Rate: 62
- Blood pressure: 80/48

I had lost about 30% of my body weight. Compare this with Karen Carpenter, the famous singer from the 1960-70s, who was 5′5″ and weighed 108 lbs. at her death. Compare this also with the normal weight range for a 5′11″ female: 140 – 171 lbs. (banner-health.com).

I was seen by a gynecologist, an endocrinologist, and later on, by a psychiatrist. A physical workup indicated all lab and X-ray values were within normal range.

Consultation and summary reports of these doctors all stated a unanimous conclusion: Anorexia Nervosa.

All noted the tell-tale signs:

- Pale
- Cachectic
- Sunken eyes
- Amenorrhea
- Emaciated
- Lanugo hair

Anorexia was not very well known by the general population in 1981, at least in Erie, PA. The condition was listed as a psychophysiological disorder in the Diagnostic and Statistical Manual (DSM-I) of mental disorders for the first time in 1952. It was mentioned very briefly under the umbrella of eating disorders (EDs). No specifics or significant explanations were given. Eating disorders were not clearly listed as a separate and distinct category until 1980, when the DSM-III was published (see DSM-III *Eating Disorders in America*, p. 324, David E. Newton). Finally, in this version, there were clear symptoms outlined:

- Fear of becoming obese
- Disturbance of body image
- Weight loss of 25% or more
- Refusal to maintain normal body weight
- No other known cause for the weight loss

The fear of becoming obese and the body image issues did not apply to me. When I looked in the mirror, I could see what was happening. I could see that I was a walking skeleton. I knew it was bad, but there wasn't a damn thing I could do about it, nor did I want to. However, the control was the thing. If I could have kept going with the rituals without losing weight, that would be fine.

Cover up with layers of baggy clothing, and no one would notice. Yeah, right.

Back to Karen Carpenter. It was not until 1983 that Karen Carpenter died of Anorexia, which brought mainstream awareness to the illness. In reading Karen's biography (*Little Girl Blue, The Life of Karen Carpenter*, by Randy Schmidt), the author covers how Karen was treated by a well-known psychiatrist. This psychiatrist had treated approximately 300 patients with eating disorders (EDs). Karen was the only fatality. She died of heart failure caused by Anorexia. She was only 32 years old. After her death, her parents and brother, Richard Carpenter, were embarrassed. Why? They had to explain to everyone how she died. Plus, by dying she broke up the music group, The Carpenters. Millions of dollars were lost from records that would never be made. How dare she die! Her death was portrayed as a major inconvenience to her family. If she was being treated by the best doctor that money could buy, given her fame and success, and she still succumbed to the illness, the question becomes: Why couldn't she have been saved? Such a talent, with a three-octave contralto vocal range. Such a tragedy, and yet another example of why this illness should not be underestimated. Someone who was a celebrity. Someone who could afford the best treatment that money can buy. It didn't work for Karen. Anorexia killed her.

Even now, 40 years later, there still is much more to be learned. Particularly, what causes Anorexia? What health risks are involved? What are the long-term effects? These questions need to be addressed in order to define and deliver effective treatment. I believe there is no one size fits all course of treatment for AN. The manifestation, progression, and relapse rate of the illness are as unique as the individual considering the neurological complexities.

Given the lack of data and ambiguity surrounding AN back in 1981, I was extremely lucky that the doctors got it right, and fast.

The doctors also recognized the comorbidities associated with AN. In a 2006 study (Blinder BJ, Cumella E.J. Sanathara VA, *Psychiatric Comorbidities of Female Inpatients with EDs, Psychosom Med.* 2006 May-June, 68(3) 454-62.), "97% of female inpatients with EDs were found to have one or more comorbid diagnoses."

Depression is the most common comorbidity (def: a co-existing health condition) affecting the majority of anorexic inpatients. Others are anxiety (which can manifest as OCD) and substance abuse. Treating the comorbidity(s) along with AN can increase the chances for a full recovery vs. repeated relapses.

In short, I had reached the stage of Anorexia where it was life threatening. The doctors had already mentioned IV nutrition if my weight went down further. It would have been so easy to just let Anorexia continue. Slow down and then shut down. It's been said we all have five exit points in our lifetime. Our soul decides which one we use to depart this earth. This was definitely one of my exit points.

It reminded me of a near drowning incident I had when I was seven years old. We were at a neighbor's house that had a large built-in swimming pool, a rarity in Erie. They also had two young daughters around my age. With my brothers and I, there were five kids in the pool. My parents had warned us to stay out of the deep end, because the three of us had not been taught to swim, or tread water.

The two little girls were superb; they were swimming and treading water in the deep end effortlessly. Since 99.9% of the time, my brothers would not play with me, I thought, *I'll go over and play with the girls. What they're doing to stay afloat looks easy, so I can do that too, like them.*

So I went over to the rope that separated the deep end from the shallow end, lifted it up, and went under it. Once I stepped under the rope, I dropped like a rock into the deep end. At first, I was surprised. Why wasn't I floating around effortlessly like the girls? While I was underwater in the deep end, rapidly sinking to the bottom of the pool, a great wave of peace came over me. I think something was with me down there. An angel or heavenly body. In addition to the peace, I felt a huge wash of love. I thought, *If I drown, that would be okay.* I actually went out of my body then because I was above the pool, looking down at everyone. I saw them relaxing in their pool lounge chairs. This is the only time in my life that the out of body thing happened. It's just like how people have described it. I saw myself underwater. I saw my brothers in the corner of the shallow end of the pool, playing and laughing. I saw my parents relaxing in their pool lounge chairs: Sly on the left and Marty on the right. Sly jabbed Marty hard and said, "Honey!" and pointed to me underwater. Marty dove in and as soon as he had me, I was back in my body. He pulled me up on the side of the pool. I was choking out water, hiccupping, gasping for air. Everyone said, "She's okay, she's okay." I think, once the drama was over, my parents were embarrassed. Or at least I felt like I embarrassed them in front of their friends. Yet all I wanted to do was play with the girls and feel included. The sense of peace while I was underwater was the same feeling that was with me at my 101 lb. point in March 1981. The peace felt beautiful. It made me unafraid to die. If Anorexia was going to kill me, then so be it. It would be okay to let go.

I was in the medical unit of the hospital for two weeks. Anorexia is an illness that is lonely beyond belief. I had two weeks to sit in my hospital room with my thoughts. During that time there were a lot of mind games playing out. *Why is this happening to me? What did I do to deserve this?*

One day I was sitting in the chair in my room looking out the window. My stomach was so empty, it felt like it was feeding upon itself. I felt miserable. The nurse brought dinner. She set the tray on the table and left. I looked at it. I lifted up the lid and saw it was a three-inch square of lasagna. Also included in the meal was a two-inch square of frosted banana cake for dessert. I distinctly remember how the food smelled and how it looked. The next thing that happened was fascinating. Some primal survival part of my brain overrode Anorexia. For the first time in over eight months my hand picked up a fork and started putting food in my mouth. I couldn't believe I was actually eating the lasagna. It felt so weird. For the first time in over eight months, Anorexia was overruled by something else. I was in total starvation mode and my body couldn't take it any longer. Something within me was able to rise up and gave Anorexia the finger.

I ate the whole meal, quickly. I don't even remember tasting it or enjoying it. It all happened so quickly. I had to sit with the sensation of fullness. I mentioned that the lasagna was a three-inch square and the cake a two-inch square, because for a person of normal size, those would be considered small portions. For me, I felt overfull to the point of nausea. I felt sick and terrified, because I had defied Anorexia, which was unthinkable. I did not think I could live with the full feeling.

Some anorexics purge after food intake, but I never did. Not once. There was never enough to throw up; it was all about self-discipline via restriction. I put the lid back on the empty plate, and sat there trying not to panic. Shortly, the nurse came back to pick up the tray. She gave me a look like, "Am I going to have to lecture you because you didn't eat your food again?" She picked up the lid and saw that the tray was empty. Honestly, she looked disappointed because she didn't get to scold me. I looked her right in the eye and said nothing. She just said, "Good," picked up the tray, and left.

After she was gone, I called home. I needed to talk to someone. I needed a lifeline. Sly answered. Lucky me.

Me: I was able to finish a meal. It was lasagna and banana cake.

Sly: Well, why don't you do that all the time then?

I hung up the phone and cried, alone with my thoughts.

On most days, I couldn't get any food in my body, period. I found creative ways to get rid of the meals that showed up three times a day, so the nurses would think I was eating. All anorexics know these games. It is part of the sickness. Truth be told, it was probably a lot easier in 1981 to hide my sneakiness. I had to be stealthy and smart about it because there weren't any other anorexics at the hospital that I could trade secrets with; I was the lone skeleton. I also wasn't exposed to social media information overload. I didn't know there were other people out there like me. I had no point of reference or comparison. I don't even recall the doctors telling me I had Anorexia to my face. I only know they diagnosed me as such after obtaining a copy of my medical records in 2020. Regardless, Anorexia is a lonely, isolating illness.

My best chance of getting rid of food was to wrap it in a napkin, and go find a trash bin on my floor to dispose of it. The nurses were always busy, so it was easy to accomplish this. I would hide the napkin in my bathrobe, and go for a stroll. When no one was looking, I put the food in the trash. The public bathroom on my floor was also ideal for throwing food away. If I could get away with going to other floors, I did that too. More trash cans to choose from. I got rid of the food, and I got to exercise. Double bonus.

Another thing I did was flush food down the toilet, either the one in my room or a public toilet on any of the hospital floors. I would have thrown food out the window if I could have figured out a way to get it open. The toilet thing was the one that got me in trouble, though. My games were called out when I finally clogged my toilet by stuffing too much food in it. The plumber had to come and fix it. That is when I started getting the looks from the nurses. They knew it was psychological. I had already suffered through eight months of constantly being hungry and exhausted. Not to mention Sly's verbal abuse. Not to mention looks and comments from kids at school. Nasty looks from the nurses weren't going to phase me. I was too far gone to care what people thought. However, it all felt like too much. I was too weak, and I just wanted it all to be over. Depression and niggling little suicidal thoughts washed over me because I thought, *Anything is better than – this!*

My weight dropped to 96 lbs. the first two weeks in the hospital. I was scared of needles. I didn't want them to stick me with an IV. It was getting to that point. No more games. Time was running out.

AN: "Way to go, girlie, you rock! I'm so proud of you. You've mastered the clever hospital games. Let's go for 95 lbs., sport!"

CHAPTER 13
LA-LA

There was a rare bright spot during my two weeks in the medical unit. Somehow, I found out that my Aunt La-La was also in the hospital. Otherwise known as Adelaide, she was Grandma's sister. Adelaide and Agatha. La-La and Grandma. I don't know how we got La-La from Adelaide but that was what everyone called her.

Oh, how fun it was to watch them interact as I was growing up. La-La had a laugh that could blow the roof off a house. When she laughed, I had to laugh too because her laugh was contagious. Her laugh could best be described as a hyper volume cackle, and she laughed often. I wanted to laugh with her all the time. It didn't even matter what she was laughing about. She would visit Grandma a lot. I remember they would sit at the kitchen table, drinking cup after cup of coffee. They would put heaping spoons of the powder creamer in their coffee, so their coffee looked almost white instead of brown. Sometimes Marty sat with them. When that happened, it was pretty much a free for all. La-La would laugh uncontrollably and say, "Marty, you made me piss my pants, I'm laughing so hard!" La-La was loud, brazen, boisterous, uncensored. She was so comfortable being her own unique self, even when pissing her pants. No apologies to anyone for who she was, ever. She never needed to apologize for her boisterousness because it was funny and endearing. And underneath it all, she was a good person with a good heart, like Grandma. I just loved La-La, and wanted to be like her. Grandma and La-La were two sister peas in a pod, La-La the loud one, and Grandma the quiet one. Two great, strong Polish women.

As a life-long heavy smoker, La-La had health issues that put her in the hospital often. A few short years later, La-La was diagnosed with terminal lung cancer. It was 1984, and I was 19 years old. I was now living with Grandma, going to college full-time and working at a part-time job at a bakery. The job paid enough to cover my school books with a little spending money left over. I was grateful that my grandma had given me a place to stay and I loved living with her while I was in college. Grandma's house was narrow and vertical with two stories and a basement. She and I lived on the first floor exclusively. My room was very small. It was just off to the side of the front room and did not have a door. There was enough room for a bed and dresser and instead of a closet, there were a few hooks on the wall to hang my clothes. There was one small window. It wasn't much, but it suited me just fine. The smallness felt cozy to me. It was my personal space. It didn't really matter how big it was.

It was in Grandma's front room that La-La came during the last stages of lung cancer. Grandma had decided to provide home care hospice for her. A hospital bed was set-up in the front room. Being in the side room right next to her, I very much felt La-La's presence. Since I didn't have a door to my room, I heard her struggling to breathe during the night, and thought, *cigarettes did that to her*. I didn't know at the time that La-La was in home hospice. I knew she was sick, but I didn't know she was dying. It didn't seem like she was in pain, so she must have been on a generous dosage of meds.

No more loud, boisterous laughs; La-La was in the final stages of lung cancer.

Grandma, God bless her, had been through this before with Grandpa, who also died of lung cancer when I was in grade school. She knew what to do for hospice care. She was a saint and of strong mental fortitude for caregiving work, even though she struggled with depression. She was the person you'd want on your side during a crisis.

One morning, I woke up, and started to get ready for an early morning class. La-La had died during the night. Her mouth was wide open. Grandma was sitting there next to her, trying to close La-La's mouth. It wouldn't close due to rigor mortis. It was April 21, 1986. La-La was only sixty when she died, but she looked much older because of her heavy smoking.

It was the first time I saw a dead person, and I didn't know what to say or do. I wish now I could have comforted Grandma, but I didn't know how. I simply had no reference point on how to show emotions, including compassion. I certainly felt it, but just couldn't express it. So, I went on to class. I sat there thinking, *Wow, is La-La really dead?* It wasn't sinking in yet. Her body was just like a shell leftover after the person leaves it. That is what really struck me, in looking at her body after she departed. It was, *Again, wow, that is La-La's body, but she sure isn't there anymore.*

Back to my walkabout at the hospital in March 1981. La-La was very much alive and her usual boisterous self. After wandering around the hospital for about an hour, I found La-La's room on the oncology floor. AN goaded me as I tried to increase my walking pace.

AN: "Way to burn calories, girlie! A whole hour! So proud of you. Remember that 95 lb. goal. Everyone is so busy, you could walk

around all day long and not get caught. It's okay to be sneaky and clever; that's part of the game. No one else gets it."

La-La had a room to herself. And lo and behold, she was there, awake. I stood in the doorway of her room, with my hospital gown hanging off of me. I said, "Hi La-La!" She took one look at me and said, "One of my titties weighs more than you."

If anyone could make me laugh at this point, it was La-La. So I laughed. It felt *good*.

CHAPTER 14

THE HOSPITAL, PART 2 –
MENTAL HEALTH UNIT

After two weeks in the medical unit, I was transferred to the mental health unit (MHU). The doctors in the medical unit had done their due diligence by running a battery of tests to rule out underlying biological issues, such as pituitary or endocrine problems. In other words, anything other than Anorexia.

Given the unanimous consensus among my doctors that my diagnosis was Anorexia, it was the logical next step. It was logical when coupled with the fact that hospital maintenance had to come to my room to unclog the food I tried to get rid of by flushing down the toilet. Not something a normal patient does.

Once the tests were concluded the diagnosis went from likely to probable.

As the endocrinologist reported:

Impression: Anorexia Nervosa.

"I think the patient gives the classic story of Anorexia in a young female, who does well in school, who feels that she has been told by her parents that she is heavy, goes on a diet and continues to lose weight. In addition, she gives many of the clinical symptoms which one finds, the amenorrhea which may precede or come after the weight loss and in her case, preceded the weight loss. Also, the constipation and the development of the fine lanugo hair. These characteristics are very common to Anorexia Nervosa. Michele has lost over forty pounds and this represents a decrease of approximately 30% of her ideal body weight. She is presently 5'11" tall and the ideal body weight for her is in the order of 140 lbs. I think that Michele's situation is very serious. She is in a life-threatening situation and the question is what can best be done to correct this. I think psychotherapy may be of benefit although that does not prove to be consistent. Also, one has to consider some form of replacement for calories and this could come as either total parenteral nutrition [IV in a vein] or possibly as nasogastric feedings [a feeding tube through the nose]. We have reached the point with her where she is reaching a critical body mass beyond which life expectancy could be decreased."

One way to describe the MHU in 1981 is to use an analogy. Remember the island of misfit toys from the *Rudolph the Red-Nosed Reindeer* Christmas animation show? None of the toys fit in anywhere, so they gathered together on an island, isolated from the mainstream.

There were no specialized centers available to treat eating disorders in Erie in 1981. Anyone with a psychological issue serious enough for 24/7 care went to the MHU. The spectrum ranged from those who looked completely normal to those who looked completely checked out. The latter group were the people who would hum, scream, or rock constantly. It didn't take long to get used to people screaming in the hallway. It became white noise. Treating it as white noise was my attempt to apply normalcy to a bizarre situation. The upside, if there was one, was that since it wasn't a treatment center specifically for eating disorders, there weren't any other anorexic patients – no one else who lived in my hell that I could trade sneaky food tricks with.

The MHU had two floors. The second floor had the really dangerous patients; they were on lockdown, both literally and figuratively. I heard all the stories about straightjackets and padded rooms, but I never knew what went on upstairs. To quote the townsman in the original 1971 *Willy Wonka and the Chocolate Factory,* "No one ever goes in, and no one ever comes out."

The patients on the first floor were the rest of us. We knew that everyone on the first floor wasn't dangerously insane, but whatever their issue, it was bad enough for them to be there. I never felt scared around the other patients, but then again, we were never alone. If something happened, a health care professional (HCP) was right there to deal with it.

I was in the MHU until such time that I gained enough weight to be safely released. The number set was 107 lbs., which meant a weight gain of ten pounds, give or take. It took three months to reach the goal. During the entire time I didn't see any other anorexic patients, or anyone who exhibited problems with food, like a bulimic. It felt surreal to be in there. At times, it felt like I was in school, because every hour of the day was scheduled for us.

A typical day in the MHU:

- 7-8 am: waking up and getting dressed
- 8-9 am: breakfast
- 9-9:30 am: morning medication preparation*
- 9:30-10 am: (15 min. with my psychiatrist and 15 min. getting my meds)**
- 10-noon: creative time (art, puzzles, crafts)
- 12-1 pm: lunch
- 1-1:30 pm: afternoon medication preparation
- 2-3 pm: group therapy with an appointed counselor***

- 4-5 pm: more creative time
- 5-6 pm: dinner
- 6-9 pm: free time aka TV watching
- 9 pm: lights out

*A note about the medication preparations. We would all stand in line at the nurse station for our medications. Many of the patients got excited when they saw the nurses preparing the meds. It was like waiting for the doors to open at Walmart on Black Friday.

**The psychiatrist was dedicated to my care, meaning he was who I saw for the entire three months (Dr. G owns chapter 19!). Having a dedicated psychiatrist vs. rotating doctors provided a comfort level. As I got to know him, it became easier to talk about my illness and why I was there.

***The counselors that led group therapy rotated in and out. There were about six of them and two really stood out for me (more on them later too). All were warm and compassionate. I never saw any of them lose their cool. They were well trained to deal with even the most difficult patients.

In short, everyone was very professional, with certain exceptions. In hindsight, given where I was, I'm not sure they knew what to do with me, or how to help me get better. They nailed the diagnosis, but the hospital didn't have a treatment plan for Anorexia. Keep in mind that this wasn't a specialized treatment center for eating disorders. They probably didn't have many reference points either, such as previous patient cases from which to determine what worked and what didn't. Ultimately, I think they decided to treat the depression, hoping that would lead to better neurological health to combat destructive behaviors.

At best, there was compassion and fortitude. A staffer would say, "This will be tough, but you can do it. We'll take it a meal at a time."

At worst, there was ignorance. A fellow patient or staffer might say, "Just go eat something."

I understood to a point how the health care providers could get irritated and frustrated with me. As an Anorexic, I had a bunch of tricks to starve myself, and didn't like others trying to pry the lid open on my secrets. It must have been hard for them to deal with me, but they didn't seem fazed by my crazy behaviors. I'm sure they had seen a lot worse. But as day after day went by without me touching my meals, it became a battle. The staff wanted to have compassion and sympathy, but they occasionally lost patience. However, the tricks were part of my illness, they weren't me trying to be difficult. I simply didn't want to eat the meal, and I didn't want anyone trying to make me eat it. I wanted to be left alone; I was mired in depression.

The ignorance was front and center in this scenario: During my first month in the MHU, I sat at a table in the recreation room one afternoon. I was meeting with a male doctor. I did not know what his specialty was or why he wanted to see me. I was still hovering around 100 lbs., which meant I still looked really bad – wasted – skeletal. Perhaps there was a curiosity factor involved, I don't know. I remember that the doctor worked at the hospital. His personality was best described as cold and very clinical. Either he wasn't trained on establishing rapport with patients, or it wasn't his strong suit.

The conversation we had perfectly illustrates the complexity of AN and society's ignorance of this illness. He asked me a few questions about my eating habits and weight. Nothing compelling enough to stay in my memory, but I was thinking, *Who is this guy and why is he here?* The one thing that did stick with me for these 40 years was a comment he made at the end of our session. He said, "I don't understand this. I sit down and have a meal. When the meal is finished, I go do something else." He spent a few more minutes lecturing me about making sure I had three meals a day, and what those meals should consist of. Then he looked off into the distance in silence like he was pondering why I was having so much difficulty around a seemingly simple task as completing a meal. My immediate thought in my 16-year-old brain was, *It's so much more complicated than that!*

And AN was *laughing.*

AN: "This doctor doesn't get my power. Hey girlie, let's get you surrounded by a bunch of these ignorant fools, and I'll be in charge forever! You'll never get the help you need, and I will take you to the grave. Don't fight me; you don't stand a chance."

To this doctor, it was black and white. Food was fuel for the body. When your body was low on fuel, you ate. When you were full, you stopped. What we call "intuitive eating" today. Food had no other purpose than serving as fuel for the body. To give us the energy we needed to live our lives and get everything done. Like when I was a kid. How I wish I could go back to that mindset.

The doctor simply didn't understand or wasn't trained on the emotional aspects around food that women in particular deal with in general, much less the extreme case of an anorexic. During Month One, I honestly didn't understand the seriousness of AN. I also knew instinctively that this doctor didn't understand Anorexia, period. His comments revealed an ignorance, similar to Sly's criticisms of "You're just refusing to eat. You want attention. You can stop this at any time."

Even today, over 40 years later, ignorance exists, despite heightened awareness. The book Strangers to Ourselves, by Rachel Aviv, was reviewed in the Wall Street Journal by journalist Elizabeth Winkler. The main character in the book, Rachel, stops eating at the age of six. She is diagnosed with Anorexia Nervosa. In her review, the journalist describes Anorexia as "...a disorder typically brought on by reading magazines that present thinness as the ideal of femininity." A doctor in Philadelphia quickly responded via a letter to the editor that described the statement as "highly reductive." The doctor went on. "The precise cause of Anorexia isn't known, and in each case, there may be a number of contributing factors, including a variety of psychological problems and genetic background." (Julia Weinberg, JD, PhD. "There is more to Anorexia Than Stick-Thin Celebrities." Wall Street Journal, 21 Sept 2022. Op-ed.)

It definitely hurt to have people treat me this way. Even though it may have been unintentional. The doctor had no clue about the impact of his words on me. He made me feel weak and defective. In my opinion, saying something like "just go eat something" was probably one of the worst things anyone could say to an anorexic, particularly in the latter stages of the illness, when the behaviors and associated thoughts that trigger the behaviors are well entrenched.

Another example, also in Month One, at the MHU:

I was in the dining room sitting with my meal. Like most anorexics, mealtime was high drama. I was lucky. Mealtime for me was a combination of:

- Nurse guidance
- Anti-depressant meds (Elavil)
- A controlled environment
- A balance of choice vs. discipline

When a nurse or social worker would sit with me to make sure I ate, I always did better, but I also resented it. Or should I say AN resented it. AN put up a good fight in the early days of my hospitalization.

AN: "Oh, I see, you think the nurses can beat me? You think these people know how to deal with me? I'll eat their lunch! And you don't get to eat anything. Just because you're in here, doesn't mean anything is going to change between you and me. This is all one big joke and you and I both know it. Just play the part; I will help you."

Imagine going through this ordeal three times a day for three months. It. Was. Hard. Work. Every day was a battle. The nurses often rolled their eyes at my behavior, but I couldn't help it. In the medical notes, the nurses wrote that I tended to stick to "diet foods," but they never pressured me or try to force me to consume larger portions, or fattier foods. And I'm grateful for how they interacted with me. It seemed just the right balance of compassion and discipline, even on the extra hard days.

I was allowed to choose from the menu freely. There was usually a short list of options in each category. For lunch, I picked a soup, salad, and half a sandwich. I mostly chose vegetables, salads, and other low-calorie items. This was allowed, probably because it was 1981. There was no eating disorder protocol. They may have thought that any food was better than no food, and as long as my weight wasn't going down, I could have what I wanted. I liked the variety because I didn't have too much of one thing to deal with.

In the MHU, meals were taken in the cafeteria. No option to eat in my room. I got in line, grabbed a tray, plate, cup and silverware. The silverware was rolled up in a napkin, just like an old school cafeteria. Interestingly, nothing was plastic. Glass dishes, cups and stainless-steel silverware. But then again, "watchers" were everywhere. An HCP would run over and grab the butter knife out of my hand in two seconds as if I was one of those who tried to do self-harm.

My psychiatrist, Dr. G, knew that with AN, external direction in regard to my caloric intake was needed, since the appetite control center in my brain was malfunctioning. It had been so long since I had eaten normally, I had no clue anymore about food intake. What constituted a normal meal? What was a reasonable portion size? How did I know when I was full? If I was full, should I keep eating, because my appetite wasn't working correctly, and my brain was giving me the wrong information?

Add to this the psychological tug of war. Extra butter on the toast would be good for my weight gain but I'd feel guilty. Same with an extra cookie, or scoop of ice cream. Leaving something on the plate was virtuous; cleaning the plate was not.

Ultimately, the daily Elavil was a key factor in re-learning how to eat again. Why? Because it lifted my depression. Things started to look and feel better. It started a chain reaction of, *I feel better, so I want to get better, so I'll try my best with this meal.* Over time, these little bright glimpses of thoughts slowly but surely began to replace the old destructive thoughts.

Thank God, because AN was vicious. The patterns were thoroughly ingrained; it was excruciatingly hard to address and change from hurtful to helpful (and healthy) behaviors. In the beginning of my hospitalization, I didn't want to change; I would have been fine with starving myself to death. AN had been talking to me for eight months. I was brainwashed. Starving myself to death felt normal. It felt virtuous to restrict and get thinner. It felt great to get on the scale and see the number go down. AN was going to make me crash and burn unless there was outside intervention.

On this particular day, I finished the lunch meal as best I could. I took my tray over to the silver cart that housed the trays and dirty dishes. It was on wheels and had rows of ledges for the trays, similar to what they used back when hot meals were served on the airlines. When you were done, you slid the tray into one of the ledges.

I put my tray away, and then for some reason, I started pulling out and examining the other trays. I don't know why I did this. More OCD. I guess I was curious about what and how much other people ate. How much did they leave behind? Why were they allowed to leave food behind and I had to eat all of mine? What if I wanted just a taste of something? Would snatching from someone else's tray be a way to try it without having to eat the whole thing? Maybe if I snatched a morsel from someone else's tray it wouldn't count. Free calories? Crazy thought patterns drove crazy behavior. I knew while I was doing it that it was a little weird, but I couldn't stop myself. If someone was watching me, they'd see a girl pulling all the dirty breakfast trays out of the silver box. And, of course, someone was always watching because I was in the MHU. Constant watching.

Sure enough, a member of the staff saw me doing the weird thing. He came up to me, put a gentle hand on my back, and said in a kind voice "Michele, we have plenty of food. You don't have to take food from these dirty trays".

I was mortified that I had been caught. If I had seen a portion of a blueberry muffin left, would I have taken it, because it would have been less calories than a whole muffin, and therefore not as bad? When was the last time I'd had a muffin, and did I even remember what it tasted like? And if I had ordered a muffin off the menu just for myself, would I have lost control by eating the whole thing, and then felt guilty afterward? Or eaten a portion, then felt guilty about throwing the rest away and wasting good food?

This was the crazy that flooded my brain every time I sat down to a meal in this place. I realized the HCP guy was still waiting for me to say something. I was so embarrassed that I'd been caught. I said, "I'm not looking for food, I'm looking for my menu paper that I left on my tray. I want to keep it." He believed me; we retrieved it, and I went on my merry way.

AN: "We are so much smarter than they are! I use OCD to keep the fun going. We got away with the game, good girl! By the way, how dare you even think about eating a bite of a muffin?"

Welcome to my world. On good days, it was purgatory. On bad days, hell on earth. Suffice it to say, I never looked through the trays again. I didn't even know what was normal vs. crazy anymore. At least I knew I could put this in the 'crazy behavior column, do not repeat'. I started to learn that since I had starved my brain, it wasn't working properly.

I needed other people to tell me what was crazy and what was normal. The intervention by the HCP guy let me know that what I was doing was not normal; it was part of the illness. Having it pointed out to me would help me stop these destructive behaviors and help pave the way to recovery. So even though it was excruciatingly embarrassing, in the long run it was necessary. The staff in the MHU knew what to do, thankfully.

The OCD component alone made me feel crazy. I still had the compulsive need to do weird, repetitive behaviors around food, and I couldn't stop it. Instead of taking granola out of a bag and putting it back over and over again, I would sit in the cafeteria and find a dozen ways to cut up a slice of tomato in my salad. I wanted to eat the damn thing, but the slice looked too big, so I had to cut it into different sizes to satisfy the OCD. After playing with the sizes and configuring them just so on the plate, I had to deal with AN telling me not to eat it, not even the smallest piece, even though everything was laid out perfectly. Sometimes I made designs with the tomato pieces, and admired the geometrical shapes – anything to avoid putting the food in my mouth and swallowing it.

Other days, I'd sit at the table, look at the food and cry. Sometimes the nurse sitting with me would be compassionate and help me. Sometimes he or she would sigh, and grow impatient with me.

Thus, in addition to the anxiety about the food, there was anxiety about whether my watcher was going to make it easier for me or harder. Some days, I lucked out, and no one sat with me.

In short, the relationship between Anorexia and food is a psychological puzzle. Hopefully the doctor sitting across from me in the recreation room became better educated about eating disorders, or at the very least, he practiced medicine that didn't necessitate further conversations with anorexic sufferers like me. He truly would unknowingly do more harm than good. Even in my starved anorexic brain, I knew he didn't get it and probably never would.

I didn't know it at the time, but I was going to have to rely on myself primarily to get better. No one was going to do it for me, nor should they. This would especially prove to be true since there was no specific Anorexic or ED treatment at the time. My treatment consisted of a combination of pharmaceutical drugs and a generalized "How are you feeling today Michele" psychiatric therapy.

The upside of my first month in the MHU was that I was beginning to learn about my illness. I learned that some of my behaviors were bizarre because I couldn't trust myself to know the right things to do to get better. I learned that I had a serious illness that wasn't going to go away on its own. The first and most important thing I learned is that my brain was starving, just like the rest of my body.

Light Bulb Moment (#1)
The brain needs nutrition to work properly.

I can't think rationally if my brain is starved. New research shows that Anorexia can and does impact brain development. (Biological Psychiatry: *Anorexia Can Lead to Dramatic Changes in Brain Structure.* David Neld. June 13, 2022.)

Once my brain started working properly and my body received the nourishment it desperately needed, I had a fighting chance against AN. Also, with the pharmaceuticals kicking in, the depression lifted gradually. The improvement was slow and steady, but definitely there. It was such a relief. The AN coupled with depression and OCD was simply overwhelming. The three prongs of the treatment plan (food, anti-depressants, and therapy) were not a luxury, they were a necessity.

As I began to climb out of anorexic hell, I began to realize that AN is an illness, but I'm *me*. I needed to find my power because I had to be stronger than the illness. My life was too important to waste on stupid, crazy food rituals. AN was *beneath* me. Once I found my power, I needed to use it to *annihilate* AN. The definition of annihilate is "to defeat utterly." It was time to take the monster bitch down. In all honesty, I didn't know if I could do it. After eight months of starvation and a lifetime of putdowns from Sly, I truly didn't know what I was capable of. I only knew that I had to try. It was either stay on Team AN and die, or do the hard stuff that I needed to do to get my life back.

The first thing I needed to do was believe that I had a chance against AN. I came up with statements to help myself prepare to get well. It didn't matter if I believed them or not at this point, I just needed to begin, by telling myself:

ME:
I am scared; it's okay.
I will be brave.
I will be strong.
I will go up against AN, the monster bitch that preys on young people.
I can and will recover from this.

A slim ray of light peeks through the dark clouds in my brain.

CHAPTER 15
INTERLUDE

I guess it comes down to a simple choice, really.
Get busy living or get busy dying.
-Andy Dufresne, *The Shawshank Redemption*, 1994

How did I wind up in the MHU? A simple question for which I had no answer. Despite my best efforts to acknowledge and accept my situation, I was in a state of shock. When I woke up each morning, the first thought I had was trying to figure out where I was and why. Then the next thought was, *You're in with all the crazy people.* I didn't think of myself as crazy. I didn't think I needed to be in there. I just had weird eating behaviors that I didn't understand. Food was a bad thing so I couldn't have it. That didn't mean I was crazy. I shouldn't be here.

Part of me watched everything I was doing and thought, *Are you fucking kidding me?* Again, I knew what I looked like. People just stared at me. I knew I needed help. And I couldn't believe it had gotten to this point.

I berated myself:

- You're smarter than this.
- You're causing a lot of problems for Marty and Sly.
- You're an embarrassment.
- You're missing out on your life because you've chosen this illness.

Good days and bad days were extreme; there was no middle ground. Just when I started to feel like I could maybe beat AN and be the annihilator, I got down on myself for *allowing* this to happen. I should have been able to fix it myself (just like the lime green bathing suit), and since I didn't, that meant I was weak.

I sat in judgment on the ignorance of those trying to help me, but didn't acknowledge or accept my own witlessness, and I was *way* too hard on myself. I didn't understand the complexities of AN. It didn't sink in that if I had kept on going the way I was going with no medical or psychiatric intervention, I would have died. I would have been part of the estimated 20% mortality rate. As a comparison, the 20% is higher than the death rate of all other *combined* causes for females 15-24 years old. Anorexia is the deadliest of all mental illness among young people. I did not comprehend the seriousness of my illness.

I knew that restricting food made me feel good. It was the only thing I had going for me; I was holding onto it like a castaway clings to a life raft. However, the good feeling was fake. Anorexia brainwashed me to think food restriction was virtuous. The whole "Look at me, I'm losing weight" thing is fake. I started to realize that the price to pay was impossible. The only thing Anorexia offered me was pain, suffering, and a slow but sure way to kill myself. Yes, it was time for a simple choice. I had to find a way to toughen up and choose; get busy living or get busy dying.

AN: *"Who are you talking to? They're poisoning you with wrong information. Do not trust them. Remember that I am the one that made all your problems go away by making you thin. Do not listen to them!"*

CHAPTER 16
THE BAKERY

"Let's do a field trip today," Kate said. Kate was part of a group of licensed social workers (LSWs) that rotated shifts to care for the 24/7 in-patients in the MHU. Licensed social workers are HCPs with a master's degree who help patients with mental health issues. A psychiatrist has a doctorate with additional training in the development of human personality. Both were part of my treatment plan in the MHU.

It was a beautiful sunny afternoon in April 1981. It was a splendid idea for Kate to take us out for a field trip, or so I thought. Kate is not the LSW's real name, but I refer to her as such because she had a strong resemblance to Kate Jackson, who was mentioned earlier as one of the actresses on the original *Charlie's Angels* television series.

I thought there would be a lot of patients excited about Kate's invitation. A get out of jail free card! A chance to get outside! But actually, the opposite was true. The MHU had an insular quality that encouraged complacency. The rules and restrictions became comfortable; just go with the flow. Going with the flow made things a whole lot easier; I was doing myself a big favor by not bucking the system. Every minute of every day was accounted for, so I could just focus on getting well. The mental health and/or effects of the pharmaceuticals may have dampened interest in doing anything beyond the normal routine for some patients; going outside was out of their comfort zone. I wanted to feel the sun on my face and breathe the fresh air, so I said, "Yes."

Only six patients, myself included, decided to venture out with Kate. One of the six patients was a young blonde girl. She was a few years younger than me, and definitely an alpha female type. I called her Veruca (Veruca Salt from 1971's *Willy Wonka and the Chocolate Factory*. Julie Dawn Cole was the child actress who played the part of Veruca – the blonde brat who was a "bad egg." Interestingly, this was Ms. Cole's most famous role; she went on to become a psychotherapist). Veruca, the blond girl patient, was the self-appointed leader of our little group. I wondered, *Why is she in the MHU?* It had to be something significant, right? The rumors circulating among the first-floor patients was that she had either set her family's home on fire, or injured a sibling to the extent that she was dangerous and had to be admitted to the MHU 24/7. I remember watching her on this sunny April day as we were outside for a couple hours. In observing her actions, expressions, and words, I saw the strong alpha personality, and I also sensed a meanness about her. I could see it in her eyes; there was something bad in her probably driving her to do bad things. However, this was all speculation because I never saw her do anything out of line.

The others within the group didn't say much. They were completely eclipsed by Veruca.

Our group started out on the field trip, which would consist of a walk around downtown Erie. The MHU was located right at the foot of State Street in the center of downtown. At the end of State Street was Lake Erie with a nice view of the Presque Isle peninsula.

Very picturesque during the spring and summer months; a frozen gray tundra during the winter. On the MHU, we didn't see much of the lake because there weren't many windows. All the more reason to get outside and enjoy the day!

At this point, I had been in the hospital for five weeks (two weeks in the medical unit and three weeks in the MHU). Some of the patients scared me, and I was still in a state of shock and disbelief. I did feel a little untethered that day, so I stayed quiet most of the time. I was relieved that Veruca ran the show. Kate was smart enough to give Veruca some rope to run with to give her the illusion she was in charge, but I'm sure she was watching Veruca as well as the rest of us closely. The last thing Kate would want would be to have runaway patients, or worse yet, violent patients in her charge out in public.

I liked Kate, and thought it was kind of her to get us out of our routine. I didn't know we could deviate from the strict schedule, so it was nice to learn there was some room for flexibility. I'm sure Kate was well prepared, should anyone "act up," but the powers that be must have thought the risk was low. I wanted to go with Kate on the walk, regardless of who else came along. And so, we walked along State Street toward the lake. We didn't see many people out and about, since it was a weekday. Most people in Erie worked at least one job to make ends meet.

Veruca said, "Look up ahead, there's a bakery; I'll buy everyone a treat." Another thing about Veruca – rumor had it she came from a wealthy family; they could afford the best care for her. She got to carry money around in the MHU. I didn't know that was allowed; perhaps Veruca had special privileges. However, a bakery set off all kinds of alarms in my brain. AN went *ballistic*.

AN: "Oh no, girl, you're not doing the bakery. Were you not listening to me when I coached you on the muffin? Baked goods

are off limits. Walk into the bakery if you want, but you are not
allowed to indulge. You are not allowed fun of any kind."

I was not ready for a bakery in the outside world; it was too soon. We went in, and everyone chose a treat, except me. I simply could not do it. Fortunately, no one in our little group said anything. I say fortunately because I was still too weak emotionally or physically to deal with drama. I was in survival mode. Also, the fact that no one said anything illustrated a small, yet not insignificant upside to being in the MHU. No one gave you shit about your stuff because they were so immersed in their own stuff.

After everyone had made their selection, we all left the bakery. Everyone had a white bag in their hand. There wasn't a place to sit and eat in the bakery, so everyone enjoyed their treat as we continued walking. Kate had chosen a white cupcake with chocolate frosting.

I watched her remove it from the bag. She peeled off the paper cup and took a big bite. I said, "How can you eat that?" The words were out of my mouth before I could stop them. It wasn't said in a judgmental or accusatory way, but an honest to God "I want to know" way. I really wanted to know. I was fascinated that she could enjoy the cupcake without any anxiety whatsoever. She was just enjoying her cupcake on a sunny spring day. As a matter of fact, so was everyone else. Whether they chose a cupcake, a cookie, a roll, whatever, they were simply enjoying what was in their white bakery bag. Everyone was nonchalant; it was not a big deal. I watched everyone, and it made me realize how sick I was. But it also gave me a glimmer of hope. If I got well, maybe I could be like them. I wanted so badly to be like them.

Back to my question, "How can you eat that?" Kate took my question at face value. She didn't hesitate (i.e. "Oh, it's the anorexic asking a food question; I need to be careful about how I respond").

She treated it as a normal question that a normal person would ask. Brilliant. She simply said, "Well, I don't have this every day, and I know I'll be hungry again for dinner in a couple hours." This was a revelation to me because Kate was thin. She enjoyed treats and was thin! She finished the cupcake, tossed the bag in the trash, and thought nothing more about it. No anxiety prior, and no guilt after. Same with everyone else. They took a few minutes to eat their treats, then promptly forgot about them, and turned their attention back to the walk. I thought, *Will I ever be able to be normal about a cupcake ever again?*

Kate told me a story about a night when she was in college a couple years ago and went out with her roommate for dinner. They had burgers and fries. After dinner, they walked to an ice cream shop for dessert. A couple of hours later, after some bar hopping, they passed a donut shop. "We were so full," Kate said, "but the donuts looked delicious. We had to stop. We both polished off two cream filled donuts with chocolate frosting and called it a night. It was unusual for us to eat this way, but we decided to indulge, and it ended up being a fun night. We didn't feel guilty about it because it was a rare treat."

There was a donut shop in Erie called Jack Frost Donuts. It opened its doors in 1929 and had the best cream filled donuts with chocolate frosting. Kate's story reminded me of how much I enjoyed those donuts as a kid. As an anorexic, nostalgic thoughts about food *before* it all started made me sad.

Jack Frost Donuts is no longer in business, but on trips back to Erie I occasionally had a donut or two. Even then, a passing thought was, *You shouldn't have that.* Not all the time, but enough to remind me to be aware and on guard. Negative thoughts about food are a slippery slope, and I know they're not good for me. There's recovery, but what happens to the AN thoughts? Where does the brain put them? Does denying myself the donut mean I'm on the way to relapse? How do I even know when I'm entering the danger zone; is it simply a matter of what the bathroom scale says?

I don't know, but I know I was grateful to Kate that day. She was the perfect example of a thin person who was normal with food. She answered my question honestly, and without judgment. It was just what I needed to see at this point in my illness. As I think back on the day, her example was as powerful as the drugs and therapy, if not more so. I saw what my future could be like if I made it out of AN Hell. I was so impressed with Kate. She was young, beautiful and kind. She was able to enjoy treats from the bakery, and I wanted to be like her. She helped me tremendously without even knowing it. This was definitely one of the good days, as I learned:

Light Bulb Moment (#2)
Food is not the enemy. It's food, that's all.

AN: "Cupcakes are the enemy. Kate shouldn't eat them, and neither should you. Kate is not as disciplined as you are. She is weak. Do not be influenced by her."

ME: "Shut-up AN. My question is valid, and I'm worthy of respect."

Thank you, Kate.

CHAPTER 17
THE PICKUP

"Would you like to go out on a date?" he asked.

Was he talking to me? I was in a mental hospital and some guy was asking me out on a date? Where were the watchers when you needed them? Was this a joke or was this guy serious? Wow, he was serious. Code red!

All of these thoughts went through my mind in the ten seconds or so it took me to look up from my lunch plate. I was sitting at a table by the wall, alone. Similar to choosing a seat at the back of the room on my first day of school in Tulsa, I liked to be on the periphery, where I wouldn't be noticed. I was struggling with my lunch meal, as usual. I didn't have the nurse companion sitting with me today, so getting the food into my mouth was more difficult. Unlike in the medical unit, I couldn't just wrap the food in a napkin and throw it in the trash. The MHU wouldn't have allowed that under any circumstances. The guy that came up to me may have been waiting for the right opportunity, and with no nurse present, there it was.

Jeff (not his real name) was standing on my left. To his credit, he was smiling, and respectful of my personal space.

"What is your name?" Jeff asked.

Once I realized he was speaking to me, I looked up and made eye contact with Jeff. My immediate thoughts were, *Is he one of the crazy ones? Is he scary crazy or okay crazy? Or is Jeff not one of us? Does he work here or is he a visitor of one of the patients?*

It was hard to tell. He looked normal. He was very tall, clean cut, with dark hair. Good looking in a Matthew Broderick kind of way. His eyes were warm and friendly. If we were in the outside world, I would definitely have been flattered, but we were in crazy land. I was truly tongue tied because this was the absolute last thing I expected in here. Since he was an unexpected situation for which I was completely unprepared, I had no clue on how to respond.

Since I couldn't categorize him, I looked around to see if any of the HCPs were nearby; there was *always* someone nearby to intervene. No one was looking our way, nor was anyone in the process of coming over to see what was going on. Ironic how a watcher came rushing over when I was perusing the used lunch trays on the cart (humiliating!), yet when this guy was trying to do a pick-up, no one was around. Where were they when I really needed them?

I didn't feel uncomfortable with him standing there. He didn't give off a bad vibe. My sense was that he was okay, whatever his name story was.

Me: My name is Melissa, what's yours? (Yes, I lied deliberately.)

Him: I'm Jeff. Do you work here?

Me: No, and I don't think I should be talking to you right now. I'm in here like everyone else trying to get better. But thank you for asking.

Him: Oh, I didn't know you were a patient. You don't look like a patient. I thought you worked here.

Me: No, I'm in here trying to gain weight.

Him: You look okay to me. Maybe when you get out we can go to lunch sometime.

Me: Maybe. I don't know how long I'll be in here.

Him: Okay. you're very pretty. See you later.

I never saw Jeff again. I never learned more details about him. I tried to find out more about Jeff by inquiring with the MHU staff. They said he was a patient, but couldn't disclose anything more due to patient privacy laws. The staff may have opted to keep him away from me, since fraternization between patients was probably prohibited. I wasn't there to get a new boyfriend; I was there to get AN off my back.

When I found out that Jeff was a patient, I went through the brief exchange again in my mind and decided it was a little creepy. Surprisingly, though, it was another of my experiences in the MHU that was of benefit to my recovery.

Why?

- Someone of the opposite sex showed interest in me and thought I looked normal. Granted, he was a patient too, but still. If I had looked horribly wasted or sick, he wouldn't have approached me.
- Unsolicited positive attention. Whether from a male or female, it didn't matter. I wasn't used to the attention. When someone in the hospital paid attention to me, it made me uncomfortable; it made me feel like I was being put on the spot because I was so used to being invisible. Over the three months that I was in the hospital, I became more at ease with people giving me their attention and showing an interest in me particularly as the depression started to lift. I started to feel better, and so attention started to feel good; I felt worthy.

- It gave me a glimpse of what my life could be like when I got out of the hospital. I could be like a normal teenager. Go out on dates, and compare notes with my girlfriends. This might actually be fun. What about parties? I was missing those too. It dawned on me that I was missing things because the AN monster bitch was robbing me of my teenage years, all of age 15 and continuing into age 16, thus far. I realized I would never get this time back, and if I didn't begin to tap into my power to annihilate Anorexia, it would continue to steal from me. I had to find a way to end AN; this was bullshit.

Light Bulb Moment (#3)
AN takes more than it gives. The sense of control is an illusion.

Yes, it had been very comforting to sit up in my bedroom at home, counting out meager amounts of granola, and drinking cup after cup of hot tea to wash it down. Congratulating myself on another food intake win before turning out the lights. It was not control; it was self-destruction.

Light Bulb Moment (#4)
The number on the scale is just a number.

A decreasing number on the scale is not always virtuous, or a sign of accomplishment. Getting thinner is so dangerous when in the grip of AN, because the number on the scale will never go up. Unlike the psychological torment of AN, the skeletal appearance is obvious. It got to the point where I couldn't hide my thinness, which became so severe that it forced Sly to grudgingly take me to the doctor. The number on the scale will never go up until recovery starts. Even then, there has to be a coping mechanism when that number increases. As an anorexic, when I got on the scale and saw that the number increased, it was *bad*, and I panicked. An HCP had to constantly remind me that gaining was not a fail or a loss of control; it was a sign I was getting better. I had to constantly be reminded that I was sick, and that recovering meant making big changes in what I did and thought.

Jeff the patient (like Kate the LSW) opened my eyes. And for that, I'm grateful. He really got me thinking. Now, I'm always grateful when good surprises happen at the most unlikely times and in the most unexpected places.

AN: "You don't need to date. Dating is a waste of time. Going on a date means you might have to eat something. Did you not hear him suggest lunch sometime? Going on a date is a distraction from your food rituals. Why would you want to fuck up our food games, when you've come this far with me? Don't fuck it up now, Michele."

ME: "Shut-up AN. I'm worthy of someone being interested in me."

CHAPTER 18
THE KINDNESS

"Are you okay?" Chris asked.

Chris (not her real name) was another one of the young LSWs on the first floor. She bore a striking resemblance to Chris Evert, the famous tennis player. She was about ten years older than me, petite, with strawberry blond hair cut very short, like a pageboy. She looked like she might have been a gymnast in school. Very healthy looking, with a slightly muscular build that still looked feminine. She was generous with smiles, and seemed to enjoy her work with the patients. I had also seen her on the same shifts as Kate. Perhaps they were friends as well as co-workers. They both had the same sunny disposition and an infinite supply of patience.

I was in my room, alone, sitting on the edge of my bed. It was late afternoon, and starting to get dark outside. Depression was weighing on me heavily, despite the 75mg daily dose of Elavil I was taking. The happy pills weren't working today. It was one of those days where the reality of my situation took its toll on my psyche. It felt like I was wearing a heavy overcoat two sizes too big that I didn't have the energy to remove, so I just let it sit heavily on me as

I slumped on the bed. It was one of those days where I felt trapped, like I was never going to get through it and there was no point in fighting. AN had the advantage, and I was drowning in my depression.

Chris was walking by my door (which had to be left open at all times). My body language made it obvious that I was having a bad day; just slumped over on my bed - defeated. Thus, her question, "Are you okay?"

My answer to her question was a brief shrug.

Chris: Do you mind if I come in?

Me: No, I don't mind.

She entered the room, and stood near me by the bed. She was very gentle with her questioning, so I didn't have any reason to get defensive, or uncomfortable with her being there. Everything about her was positive. Happy energy rolled off of her in waves. If I hadn't been so mired in my bad mood I would actually have been jealous.

Chris: Would you mind if I pulled up a chair and sat with you?

Me: No.

We sat in companionable silence for a while.

Me: I'm so tired of doing this.

Chris: Yes, this must be very hard for you.

Me: My mother never comes to see me.

Chris: I know. I'm so sorry. That is not your fault.

Me: I feel like it is.

During the three months I was in the hospital, I didn't get many visitors, and that in itself was depressing. Marty visited once or twice a week, the most of anyone. My brothers did not come to visit at all. I thought the reason they didn't visit was because they were uncomfortable going into a mental health unit, and probably didn't know what to say to me. I found out later from Mick that Sly told him no visitors were allowed, which was an outright lie. Of course, visitors were allowed. Sly lied to Mick and Mark, so they were kept in the dark about what was going on with me.

Sly came to visit one time. She brought her friend Stella because she didn't want to come alone. It was easier to have a buffer. I knew Stella well. She was in her early fifties; about 15 years older than Sly. The age difference was nothing in comparison to the difference in their personalities. Stella was kind, generous and funny, as opposed to Sly's coldness. Despite the age and personality differences, they worked together at a supper club in downtown Erie, and probably bonded over that. I liked Stella very much, and got to know her better over the summer when I was 11 years old. She taught me how to play tennis. Stella loved the game, and I loved it too once I started playing. She was very patient and encouraging, particularly since I'm a left hander and she was a right hander. She made sure to show me the left-handed positions for serving, forehand, and backhand even though that wasn't how she played. Stella was a competitive league player, and taught me the basic fundamentals of the game. Once I had those down, we were able to play. I got better and better by practicing with her.

Based on what Stella taught me, I developed a killer backhand and was able to make the high school tennis team in my junior year. Tennis became an enjoyable alternative to the basketball I had given up in my sophomore year when the coaches were afraid I was going to fall over on the court. Unfortunately, there were only four people on our team. In my senior year, we couldn't get enough players, so the team was cancelled. Students in the burnout schools like Tech had other priorities. Tennis was too nerdy, too wholesome for the student body of Tech Memorial. They'd rather roll a joint behind the building after school than hit the tennis courts.

On the day Sly and Stella came to visit, we all sat at a table in the recreation room. Stella kept looking at me, shaking her head and saying, "I can't believe this happened to you." Her face was full of compassion and she looked like she might cry. I thought, *Why can't you be my mother?* Her reaction was a 180 from Sly's, "I can't believe I have to take you to the doctor" commentary said with great irritation.

I laughed to myself and thought, *Stella, I could not agree with you more!* Throughout the day, I would frequently say to myself, *I can't believe I'm in the psych ward. I can't believe this has happened to me. How did this happen to me?* My self-conversations were tenfold over what I ever said in public. I just sat there, trying to stay composed, and thanked Stella for coming to visit me. I wondered how she even got Sly to agree to the visit, as Sly would never have *initiated* it. Sly broke her own rule of not allowing visitors to come see me; perhaps Stella was persistent. Although I was grateful and appreciate of Stella's visit, I continued to go down the path of negative thoughts, my mood would plummet, and depression became so much worse. It was not good for my recovery, obviously, because it was all negative self-talk.

AN: "You're in the psych ward because you couldn't convince your family that thin is beautiful. They don't get it. Neither does Stella; she hasn't seen you in a while and should be congratulating you instead of sitting there in disbelief.

Sly sat at the table with Stella and showed no emotion whatsoever. Sly had no parenting style; she was hyper-critical, finding fault in everything I did. Really, her thorough approach to the destruction of my self-confidence was remarkable. Marty and Sly's parenting agreement was that Marty would raise the boys and Sly would raise the girl(s). Lucky me. While the whole Anorexia thing was going on, Marty was hands off. Marty and Sly also chose not to share anything about my illness with Mick or Mark. They could not visit me; they didn't know anything about what was going on with me other than I wasn't home. How sad. Even though Marty came to visit me regularly, I was not his responsibility to raise. He was upset that I was sick, but he chose to stay in his lane; he didn't want to incur the wrath of Sly. I think he regretted his choice later in life. The thing about regret is that you can't go back and re-do the thing you regret, or wish you had handled differently. Either try to fix it with the person you hurt, or let it go.

Nevertheless, the fact I had become a walking skeleton, and was in the MHU 24/7 was an indicator that the parenting plan was not working too well. But what does a 16-year-old know? I got to see my brothers when I was allowed to go home on weekends. Home visits were allowed near the end of my hospitalization *if* I was on track with my weight gain. Those weekends gave me the opportunity to "practice" eating at home, to make sure my new, healthy habits were sticking.

At any rate, neither Marty nor my brothers played a significant part in my recovery. And with Sly being incapable of helping me in any way, shape, or form, it was up to me to decide. Did I want to get better or not? The answer changed every minute of every day, but I kept trying. On this particular day, sitting in my room, waiting for the call to dinner, I didn't feel very strong. The negative thoughts were getting the better of me. I felt abandoned and alone. Dumped in the looney bin. Poor me.

The staff was aware of Sly's absence and documented "the mother issue" in my case records. Per Chris's comment, I sensed they felt sorry for me. What mother doesn't visit her child in the hospital, especially when the child's illness is life threatening?

Veruca's mother visited her all the time, despite Veruca's being a pyromaniac and sibling beater (disclaimer: theories shared by the majority of MHU Floor 1).

What was wrong with me?

During my 16 years, I didn't know what it was like for someone to sit with me and give me their undivided attention. I didn't feel like I was deserving of Chris' attention. Why was she spending her time sitting with me and being nice to me? It was such a novel thing; I simply didn't know what to do or how to act. When someone was proactive in giving me attention, I became anxious, because the behavior was out of my comfort zone, especially if it came from people in the MHU I didn't know. Being the recipient of attention was so foreign to me that I immediately became anxious and self-conscious. AN was brilliant in recognizing these moments and continued to hammer away.

AN: "Oh look, Chris feels sorry for you. Sweet little heart-to-heart conversations with the staff aren't going to help you. What a waste of time. You're not listening to me, and that's why you're depressed. You're such a pathetic loser."

After Chris said, "It's not your fault," I started to cry. She continued to sit with me. There was no judgment; Chris simply held space. It was glorious. I had never had this kind of interaction with anyone before. She didn't have to sit with me. There were other things she could have been doing. But she chose to spend time with me, and genuinely wanted to do what she could to help me feel better.

It was pure kindness. It was emotional sunshine pouring onto me. Once I got past the *newness* of it, I basked in the warmth of it. The heavy overcoat of depression started to feel a little bit lighter. Finally, Chris took my hand, and we walked to the cafeteria for dinner, together.

There are a lot of things I don't remember about my three months in the MHU. I don't remember much about the food I ate, whether I slept well, or what I wore. What I remember best were those acts of kindness from people that didn't know me. What they said, their expressions, and their positive outlook were game changers for me. A little went a long way. Not only was it beneficial at the time, but the benefits also continued long after I left the hospital. Those moments helped to change my thought patterns, which ultimately helped me to beat AN. I will always remember how Chris took the time to try and help me feel better. Even though it was only one time, and of short duration, the impact on me was huge.

AN: "She's paid to check in on you, idiot."

ME: "Shut-up AN. I'm worthy of someone showing me kindness."

Thank you, Chris.

CHAPTER 19

DR. G

Now, I want to introduce the psychiatrist assigned to my case - the mighty Dr. G.

For a visual of Dr. G, imagine a combination (looks-wise and personality-wise) of Anderson Cooper and Mr. Rogers.

One of the first things I noticed was the hard time I had talking to him. Why? During my sessions with Dr. G, I learned that part of my aversion to attention was middle child syndrome. Psychologically speaking, a middle child often feels left out, ignored, and not heard. On the plus side, however, the middle child also tends to be independent as a result. Research aside, suffice it to say that I wasn't used to talking about myself. Sitting in a session with Dr. G forced me to focus on myself. He was trained to make me think about myself. I had never been to a psychiatrist before, so I had no frame of reference (which was good). I felt like I had to answer in a certain way; I wanted to be the *good girl*, and get his approval.

Dr. G came to the MHU from his private practice twice a week. As one of Dr. G's in-patients, I stood in line waiting to see him twice a week in the morning. There were ten of us, and we each had a session of 15 minutes with him. It was like a psychiatric drive-through express lane. Put in your order, get your pills. I got a paper cup with five dark colored pills and three light colored ones (twice a day). A part of me wondered, *What is the point of all this?* It felt like a very "one size fits all" type of psychiatric treatment.

I figured the professionals knew what they were doing; what other choice did I have? Again, back in 1981, there weren't any specialized eating disorder treatment centers. The nation's first residential eating disorder facility, The Renfrew Center, opened in 1985 in Pittsburgh (www.eatingdisorderhope.com). No one even talked about weird eating habits. No one knew how to treat Anorexia. As a result, my meds plus therapy treatment were very generalized.

To an observer, it's a puzzling illness. People don't understand. Again, the ignorance of, "You're skinny, why don't you eat more?" To sufferers, it's hell on earth. AN is a sneaky, insidious, subtle illness that destroyed my mind, body and spirit. AN made me feel like I was a good dieter at the beginning. Over time, I became addicted to the control aspect. The subtleness was the most dangerous part; a pound here, a pound there, no big deal. Until one day I woke up, and had lost 30% of my body weight. The ease with which AN got out of control in my case was scary, which is why AN is dangerous and deadly. No one should have to go through it.

Dr. G always started off with:

"How are you feeling today?"

It's funny to think about now. I'm an in-patient in a mental hospital with crazy people. My parents signed me in and I can't leave. I look like a skeleton. All I have is 15 minutes, tops, to talk about how I'm feeling and try to get this AN monster bitch off my back and out of my head.

"How are you feeling today?" What an interesting question for an anorexic. A few years ago I was at my local gym. I was working out on one of the weight machines. A personal trainer walked by.

Right behind him came an older gentleman. It was obvious they had just finished a workout session. The trainer said, "How do you feel?" The guy said, "Compared to what?" I wish I had used the same answer with Dr. G. How perfect. Compared to what, collapsing of starvation, and dying on the floor? Compared to that, I'm doing amazing, thank you for asking.

Dr. G's initial impressions, per his 1981 clinical notes:

"She has had no surgery. She has had no serious illnesses. She does not use alcohol, tobacco, or street drugs. She considers herself somewhat of a loner. She is a follower and not a leader. She is a worrier. She is sensitive. She is perfectionistic. She is punctual. She is religious. She is able to get her feelings out."

When I read those notes for the first time via a copy I obtained in 2020, I didn't completely agree with his assessment. I wasn't a loner because I always had my basketball girlfriends. Whether I was a leader or follower had yet to be determined. I'd like to think I was a leader. Doesn't the above sound a lot like kids today who are on social media all the time? Playing X Box et al? The point being that the condition of Anorexia can manifest no matter how much or how little digital information is saturating the individual. The digital piece definitely does not help; it can lead to excessive isolation, which is not good for mental health.

AN: "That's right, girlie. I use it to brainwash kids. Have you heard of the pro-ana movement? It's a bunch of websites that offer content and images that encourage people to aspire to anorexic bodies. It is my pride and joy. If you're not skinny, you're a worthless piece of shit."

I was, however, highly impressionable, as are most teenagers. Dr. G was the voice of authority. If he said it, I went along with it, whether or not I agreed. He was the doctor. I was the patient. It was so much easier to go along with the rules in the MHU vs. trying to resist (as an extreme example, Jack Nicholson's character in *One Flew Over the Cuckoo's Nest* who is forced to undergo a lobotomy for causing trouble).

It was early April 1981. In his consultation report, Dr. G agreed with the other doctors who examined me in that the correct diagnosis should be Anorexia Nervosa. He also agreed to continue seeing me, and did so throughout my hospitalization. In fact, he was my only psychiatrist; there were no others involved, which somehow made this part of my treatment easier.

AN gleefully laughed and mocked Dr. G's assessment.

AN: "I knew these things about you two years ago, when Sly called you fat. You were perfect for Team AN. I taught you control, accomplishment, discipline. I showed you how thinness is the answer to everything. Dr. G doesn't know what he's talking about; how can a man know the pressure a woman faces to look good in today's world? He's no match for me."

Dr. G was also my grandma's psychiatrist. He treated her for depression, which she had suffered for decades. When I had my sessions with Dr. G, I always asked him how Grandma was doing. "Now, Michele, you know I can't talk to you about your grandma's treatment," Dr. G said. "Every patient session is confidential. But she talks very fondly of you all the time." Again, very Mr. Rogers-like, with his soft voice and gentle manner. I was too young to know about HIPAA (The Health Insurance Portability and Accountability Act of 1996) privacy rules and he politely declined to share anything no matter how hard I pressed him. I was too young to know about patient confidentiality. But it was my grandma, for God's sake.

The fact he treated my grandma was enough in and of itself for me to feel comfortable with him. When I met him in early April, I was still shell shocked with my whole situation. I had only been in the hospital for about a week, and had not yet moved from the medical unit to the MHU.

The other thing I liked about Dr. G was his calm demeanor. He didn't judge me. His approach worked very well for me. The calm approach was good for someone like me who grew up listening to my parents scream and fight with each other, or yelling and hitting me. There was too much violence at home. Dr. G asked questions, and actively listened to everything I had to say. He did his job very well; I thought he was so damn smart. Dr. G came across very authentically. He was one of those people that matched their profession perfectly. I usually felt better after my brief sessions with him twice a week. Perhaps Dr. G had a good plan for treating me because he already knew a lot about our family from Grandma. She may have shared some of the family dynamics with him, and therefore he had a better picture of what led up to me sitting there in his MHU office. I didn't care, I was just glad it was a good fit between us.

It didn't take me long to trust Dr. G. I started telling him about how the AN voice was working constantly in my head, trying to sabotage everything I was trying to do to get well. The soundtrack that repeated the most, went something like:

AN: "Don't eat that. You cannot eat that. If you eat it, I will make your life a living hell. I will heap so much guilt on you that you won't ever think of defying me ever again."

Constantly. Relentlessly. It overrode my growling stomach every single time, every minute of every hour of every day.

Dr. G said, "You're hearing voices?" He perked up and started writing furiously on his notepad. "How often are you hearing these voices? Can you elaborate?"

"No," I said, "it's not voices. It's just my brain telling me not to eat, and threatening me with tremendous guilt if I give in. It's easier for me not to give in and stay hungry. Every time I try to fight against AN it's so hard. AN tries to talk me out of doing the things I need to do to get better. AN sabotages me out of every fucking positive thought I might have. It's exhausting, and every day is a battle."

When I got on a roll, I would always start crying, because it *was* hard. Every minute of every hour of every day.

Dr. G nodded and went back to his calm demeanor. It was almost funny to see Dr. G go down the path of schizophrenia with the, "Why are you hearing voices" questioning, before checking it off the list. The man was thorough, no doubt. I would have been so drugged up on hardcore schizophrenia meds it probably would have drowned out AN. Or better yet, if they'd given me something to turn me into a zombie, I would have gone along with food intake all day long. AN recovery is so excruciatingly hard that it makes psychotic drugs look appealing.

Back to Grandma. She died in 2005, and I never knew what caused her depression. It was bad enough that she had electric shock treatment therapy in the 1960s. I asked her about it once. She said it erased parts of her memory. She never seemed to regret having, what some would call, controversial treatment. This was before anti-depressant pills became mainstream. Once those were available, she had them prescribed and stayed on them the rest of her life.

With her history of clinical depression, it seems Grandma was well qualified to share with me the following statement. "There is something wrong with your mother. I wish your dad had married Nancy. That was his girlfriend before Sylvia showed up. She was tall, blond, and so nice. We got along so well. Your mother went after your dad when her current boyfriend moved out of town. And then your dad dropped Nancy." Grandma told me the same story many times over the years.

Sitting in Dr. G's office in the spring of 1981, I had no way of knowing that in a few short years, I'd be living with my grandma. She would provide further context around Sly. When Grandma was telling me stories, it wasn't to gossip or be malicious. I think she was hurt by how Sly treated her. I was also old enough to hear these stories, which helped to fill in the blanks on Sly's inability to be a parent. Lucky for me, Dr. G had me on Elavil twice a day. AN plus the comorbidity of depression equals darkness. In my case, throw in the OCD too. No wonder I needed the meds so badly. My crying usually started when I told Dr. G about Sly. How she hit me, berated me and made me feel like nothing I did was good enough. I told him about the time I was ten years old, in bed sleeping. I was lying on my side. Sly came in and started karate chopping me on my waist. She was hitting me hard and it woke me up. *What the fuck?* That was one of the scarier moments, when I wished she would take her rage out on someone else.

Dr. G's Note:

"I feel that the patient should have some family involvement in her therapy. Whether or not the conflict with the mother is primary or secondary, this must be dealt with."

He worked diligently to get Sly to come in for counseling as well. She refused. In the end, it was probably better. The dynamic between us was never going to change. Why not just focus on getting better vs. complicating the recovery with the impossible goal of a loving mother-daughter relationship?

So, that's what I did.

CHAPTER 20
FRISBEE

Winter turned into spring. Looking out the window at MHU, new life was sprouting everywhere. The late winter, with all of its cold gray slushiness, was being replaced by fresh green buds, and more sunshine. The days were growing longer. Erieites breathed a sigh of relief when winter was over.

The thaw was the only indicator I had that time was passing. Inside the MHU, life looked and felt the same. The long, slow road to recovery continued. I was still plagued by distorted thoughts, and I understood this. It was never the case where I looked at myself and thought I needed to lose more weight. I didn't like gaining weight, but I knew it was necessary. I had to learn to deal with feelings like guilt, anxiety, fear and anger. It was the first time in my life where I was forced to deal with my feelings. It was particularly difficult when I got dressed in the morning. If I put on a pair of jeans, and they felt a little tighter, I used to get upset. I had to work really, really hard to replace those negative emotions with something positive, like, *I'm getting healthier.*

Regardless of whether it was my thoughts or AN sabotaging me, my body felt better. No more heart palpitations, trouble breathing, or bone crunching fatigue. It just felt, holistically, that I had hit rock bottom in the medical center, and now the only thing to do was get on the road to improvement. The alternative to staying at rock bottom in perpetual starvation mode, or worse dying, was no longer an option, despite the seductive pull of AN. I still couldn't distinguish between the "ME" thoughts and the "AN" thoughts. I had to have faith that the HCP team at the MHU would keep me from going off the rails, and as hard as it was, I had to have faith in myself that I could pull this recovery off. Although I didn't know about relapse, and no one ever discussed it with me, I knew intuitively I could *not* go through Anorexia again. It *had* to be a one and done. It had sucked so much out of me; another round would have done me in.

I wasn't starving my body anymore. Like the lasagna and banana cake, the meals I had were smaller portions than what I would eat when I got back to a suitable weight (140-150 lbs. for a 5'11" female) but the three meals a day plus snacks helped my body heal. My body and brain were beginning to operate better. I wasn't in survival mode anymore, even though I was still severely underweight. It was almost like my heart was saying, "Code red has passed; her body functions can move out of panic mode and work on getting back to normal."

I felt a great deal of guilt most days about my situation, which was a driver in my desire to get better. The fact I had to be in the hospital was an embarrassment to my family. It shouldn't have been, but in Erie, PA that's how it worked. It was all about appearances. Again, the culture in Erie was one of putting on the appearance that all was well; no one aired their metaphorical dirty laundry. It was similar, in a way, to today's online postings where everyone is happy and life is perfect. Completely unrealistic, then as now. It was shameful for the family to deal with the whole "Where's Michele" thing. I felt guilt for putting this on them. I felt embarrassed for embarrassing them – that middle child thing, again. Don't make waves. Ever.

On this spring day, it was particularly warm and sunny. The staff advised that any patients on the first floor were allowed to go outside. We could go out in the back of the MHU building - supervised of course. The backyard looked like a space where kids would have recess. Picture a well-kept rectangular stretch of green lawn with a fence and a few trees around the perimeter, with Lake Erie clearly visible. Whoever the landscaper was that took care of the lawn did an outstanding job. The grass looked like the kind of velvety stuff on golf courses. No wonder some patients were taking off their shoes off to run through it. All in all, this was very good for everyone's mental state, it seemed. Smart staffers at the MHU, indeed.

I was taking all of this in from the industrial kitchen on the MHU first floor. All the meals for the first-floor patients were prepared in-house. I saw some patients playing frisbee and it looked like fun. As I stood in the kitchen, I realized how quiet and deserted it was inside the building. It was after lunch, and no one, I mean *no one*, was around. There must have been a mass exodus to the outside. This was common in Erie, PA, as the winters are brutal and can last up to six months. Snow squalls come across Lake Erie from Canada (known as the "lake effect"), and bury the city in snow from October through March. At the first sign of spring, people cannot wait to get outside.

I was suddenly overwhelmed by the feeling that I was missing out – *on everything*. Watching people have fun made me sad. Why? I was beginning to realize how Anorexia took over my life and left me with nothing. I couldn't see this during the eight months I was starving myself since I was self-isolating. It was easy to starve alone. Alternatives were not in my face, whereas other options were made available at the MHU – a walk to the bakery or a game of frisbee. I still had a choice; I could still say "no", but if it was either staring at the walls in my MHU room, or going out and doing something, I'd rather force myself to start to socialize. If those other people who had various kinds of mental illness could go outside and enjoy themselves, then I had a right to partake also.

On this spring day, I had the desire and energy to go outside. To play. To try and remember what it was like to have fun and feel joy. I felt like a very old sixteen-year-old who had gone through an emotional shredding machine. All the good stuff was torn away and there was nothing left. Getting my energy back in small increments was key. Fortunately, I was no longer cold all the time. The fine lanugo hair on my arms was gone. Getting out and enjoying the fresh air seemed so appealing.

It was like a metaphor for my life. I was wasting away in the MHU while the world moved on. Again, I had the sensation of being young and missing out on all of the fun. It was not a good feeling.

Light Bulb Moment (#5)
AN was causing me to miss out on my life.

Light Bulb Moment (#6)
I refused to play the victim because AN happened to me.

As I passed through the MHU kitchen on my way to the back-yard, I saw a rack filled with trays of vanilla cupcakes that were cooling. Interesting how cupcakes were part of a pivotal moment in my recovery for a second time. On another rack was a tray with a large bowl of vanilla buttercream frosting. Someone was going to frost the cupcakes as soon as they were cool enough. Since it was later in the afternoon, the cupcakes were the night's dessert option after dinner. I stopped at the racks, and caught the wonderful aroma of the freshly baked cupcakes. Without thinking about it, I stuck my finger in the frosting bowl. It tasted amazing. I couldn't believe no one was around watching me. It was so regimented at MHU, I thought someone was going to catch me licking the frosting. No one did, and I went outside. I ran. I played frisbee. I started living again.

I was learning how to be me. I couldn't go back to being a child, and I couldn't remain an anorexic. I had to find *me*. I remember standing in the kitchen, thinking, *Life is passing me by out there. I've got to get on with it, whatever it takes. I don't want to miss out on my life anymore.* AN was still hovering around in my brain, but the monster bitch's power wasn't as strong on this day. Maybe the bitch was off recruiting some other innocent, impressionable kids. Today, I was winning. It felt good to be outside. It felt good to play frisbee when, a few months ago, I barely had the energy to dribble a basketball at practice. Instead of lying in bed, feeling depressed, refusing to eat, I was beginning to socialize more and enjoy it. Baby steps. Plus, lying in bed feeling depressed was not an option at MHU. As a 24/7 MHU patient, I wasn't free to do what I wanted; I had to follow the rules. I'd often heard other patients complain about the rules, but I didn't have a problem with them. They were the means to the end, which was getting better, not only so I could leave, but also to ensure I'd never have to come back again.

Continuing with the cupcake theme, the very next year, at seventeen years of age, I'd get a job at a mom and pop German bakery. Colonial Bakery was well known in Erie, and especially popular for its 100% pure whipped cream cakes. The main location was just three blocks down the road from my college. It was the kind of old school bakery where customers would get in line and take a number from a paper ticket holder. Glass cases took up most of the store and showcased the desserts, breads, donuts and pastries (similar to Carlo's bake shop, where the "Cake Boss" became famous). Lines formed out the door on weekends and during the holiday season. Back in the 1980s, mom and pop bakeries were common. The ones still in operation should be celebrated; they are unique. The recipes are passed down through generations of family. At Colonial Bakery, the recipes were kept in a locked safe. Only the owner and the employee who made the recipe had access. These types of bakeries are gems.

Yes, for the next six years working at Colonial Bakery, I would occasionally swipe a finger scoop of buttercream frosting before anyone saw me. Actually, they saw me and didn't care. The frosting was mixed in an industrial mixer. When fully mixed and fluffy, it was put into a silver cylinder that looked like a large garbage can. The frosting was decadent. It also made my hands nice and smooth because of the butter content. Everyone who worked at Colonial Bakery was kind of like a big family. If someone saw me take a swipe, they'd just wink.

I'd go on to multiple other jobs in my adult life, from entry level paper pusher to high paying power career, and everything in between. Colonial Bakery was my favorite; I thought all jobs were fun like that. Sadly, Colonial Bakery no longer exists, but sometimes I have dreams where I'm back there working, and everything looks and smells exactly like it did circa 1982. In my dream, it's the busiest time of the year, between Thanksgiving and Christmas. Customers are lined up out the door. Everyone takes a number from the paper ticket machine and waits their turn. Everyone is in a good mood, laughing and talking. People are connecting with other people in real time; there are no cell phones.

In my dreams, I smell what is baking in the ovens. Breads, cakes, sweet rolls. It all smells wonderful. The ovens are going non-stop, which makes the bakery warm and inviting to customers, given the holiday snow outside. I can even see how everything is arranged in the glass cases on light pink trays. There are racks upon racks of goodies in the back waiting to replenish the cases as soon as they sell out. If I ever had a bakery of my own, I would do the exact same layout as Colonial Bakery.

It's been said that the most important part of dreams is not necessarily what you see in the dream, or who you are, but how you *feel*. I always feel so happy in my Colonial Bakery dreams. I welcome that dream as often as my subconscious wants to release it.

CHAPTER 21
DEPRESSION AND GUILT

Anorexia Nervosa is a very lonely illness. The self-imposed isolation becomes more and more prevalent as the illness progresses. Parties, events, dinners and socializing in general are off limits, not only because food is part of those things, but also because it's too exhausting to go anywhere or do anything. Then there are the surprised, and sometimes, judgmental looks from people I preferred not to encounter. Why go through all of that when I didn't have to? It was all I could do to get through the day without collapsing from hunger and weakness.

At night when I got into my bed with my cup of hot tea, I would often cry with relief that the day was over. I could let my emaciated body and mind rest. I could finally get warm under many layers of blankets. I had made it through another day. Slipping into sleep was a delicious escape I looked forward to – another stark example of how AN with underlying depression is like a nightmare. As this dreadful illness took hold and ultimately took over, the depression rode sidecar with it, and made everything look worse than it really was. I felt trapped; I was in the deep forest in my brain, with no compass to guide me, and no idea how to escape.

Every time Sly said something hurtful like, "You're fat," and, "I can't believe I have to take you to the doctor," it felt like an emotional sucker punch to the gut, and exacerbated the depression. I really just wanted to die. Truth.

Anorexia is a fucking roller coaster. Belt yourself in and hang on, or you'll free fall and be destroyed. As the reality of my situation started to sink in, I became more depressed. I didn't think my options for moving forward with my life were very attractive. Tossing a frisbee around one day, feeling strong. Then waking up the next day and feeling despair, telling myself I was never going to get better and wanting to die.

Over the course of the three months, I thought about death often. There were times where it seemed like a very appealing option. *Anything,* even death, would be better than *this.* Why? Because AN is exhausting on every level – physically, mentally, spiritually. It's like being pulled in by a riptide. By the time I realized I was in it, I was too worn down to even think about trying to get out of it. The riptide is too powerful. It was easier to let it suck me under, and I thought, *Okay, well I'll just go peacefully.* My brain was saturated with thoughts such as these on bad days in the MHU.

On one particularly hard day, the nurses' station told me I had a phone call. This was surprising. Patients didn't get many phone calls, and visiting hours were limited.

I took the call, and was even more surprised Sly was on the other end, especially since she never called or visited. She wanted nothing to do with me, so why was she on the phone calling me? And it was later in the day. Sly would have been getting ready to go to work as a cocktail waitress at the upscale supper club where she worked with Stella, my superb tennis teacher.

Marty didn't like Sly working. Sly would get all dolled up and take off around four o'clock in the afternoon before he got home from work. If she was still there when my brothers and I got home from school, she was ready to head out the door, and didn't acknowledge us. I remember watching her head out the door for work. She had so much makeup on that she looked clownish. Lots of face powder, and big circles of rouge on her cheeks. Bright red lipstick and blue eyeshadow. I asked her once why she wore so much makeup to work, and she said the restaurant was dark so she had to wear more. She also wore a black cocktail waitress outfit, consisting of a skirt, vest, white shirt, black pantyhose, and black shoes.

She would be excited as she headed off to work, like she was getting ready to go to a party. Who knew what went on down at the club? And why the gobs of makeup, really? Especially since the supper club closed at 11:00 pm, and she didn't get home until around 2 in the morning. What was going on between 11:00 pm and 2:00 am?

When she got home, she'd sit in bed crunching through a bag of potato chips with the light on. I guess she needed to wind down after the party. Meanwhile, Marty had to get up in four hours for work – another strike against Sly's job. I know why she did it. She needed some excitement in her life, and this was her chance to get out, meet people, perhaps flirt, and still feel attractive. This was when we were in grade school, so Sly and Marty would have been in their early to mid-thirties, still young by today's standards, yet with three kids already in our teens.

Back to the phone call. Here's how it went, verbatim:

Me: Hello?

Sly: If you don't stop this, your father and I are getting a divorce.

Me: What?

Sly: Do you know how much money this is costing us?

She yelled this at me, and then hung up. I suspect Sly and Marty probably had multiple fights over my situation and the phone call was probably triggered by one of them.

Shouldn't I have been used to this after 16 years? No, I never got used to it. Another emotional sucker punch. Go to your pattern, Michele. Feel the pain in your gut. Feel the tears start and make them stop. Stuff it down, suck it up and don't be so sensitive. I didn't yet know how to toughen up and let it roll off of me. I wouldn't dare talk back to her because that's when she'd hit me. I was conditioned. Great work, Sly and Marty. I couldn't just let it go (that is, until I hit my thirties and went into heavy duty therapy). I thought she had called to see how I was doing.

And so again something more within died. What? My dream of what a mother should be and my stubborn hope that one day she might say something nice to me.

In one of the psychological evaluations, the case worker wrote:

"The parents give sketchy information regarding family history, however the father admitted that there have been ongoing marital problems, which apparently include Michele because [of] the parents' conflict regarding how they act toward and manage Michele."

A healthy dose of guilt got sprinkled into my depression soup. Beautiful.

Slowly, and painfully, I came to the realization that food restriction was not the answer, and it would not fix the problem. What problem? Family dysfunction, depression, genetic code, susceptibility, who knows? But whatever it was, it had to be fixed.

The realization made the depression worse for a while. I thought, *If I don't have the comfort and security of food control, what else is there? What the hell do I do without it?*

Again, I felt guilty for being a big "family" problem, causing a rift between my parents, and costing them a lot of money. I wasn't worth all this trouble, or so Sly would have me believe. She would have me believe that the family would go bankrupt because of me. There was no money for my recovery. Truly a big burden for a 16-year-old to carry around.

Neither Marty nor Sly ever told me how much my hospitalization cost. Years later, I brought it up with Marty. He told me there was only the deductible to pay; his employer's health insurance covered the rest. If that was true, why would Sly try to make me feel guilty about it? Why project her abnormal thriftiness onto me, and make me feel like it was my shortcoming and not hers? I don't know, but this is what therapy is for.

In the end, the Elavil and counseling helped get me out of the emotional despair. Once I got out of the dark, my perspective started to shift for the better. This occurred about halfway through the three months. Yes, Sly was badgering me, trying to make me feel bad about still being in the hospital. But the health care professionals around me helped me to see her behavior more objectively. They helped to create a tiny wave in my sea of conditioning.

I couldn't control what Sly said or did, and I couldn't change her. But I didn't have to starve myself to death. A slight shift in my thinking occurred.

Light Bulb Moment (#7)
Having Anorexia Nervosa doesn't make me defective.

A statistic to crystallize the thought:

The number of young women between the ages of 15 to 19 who have Anorexia Nervosa has increased every 10 years since 1930 (www.hopkinsmedicine.org/health/conditions-and-diseases/eating-disorders/anorexia-nervosa).

Young people. Not defective, just hurting. The numbers are getting larger.

CHAPTER 22
DISCHARGE

It was June 1981. I not only had reached my goal weight of 107 lbs., but had also exceeded it by five pounds. I had finished treatment and could go home. As the day for discharge grew closer, questions were rapidly filling in my head:

- Am I recovered?
- What does recovery mean?
- Is it a number on the scale, or something more?
- If something more, then what is that, and do I have more work to do?
- If I have more work to do, let's call it X, Y and Z. If I don't do X, Y, and Z, will I relapse?
- Is recovery a lifelong thing, or can I be called cured and go back to the way I was before AN?
- What is normal eating, and how do I know if I'm doing it *right*?
- What is skinny?
- What is fat?

- Will I ever be able to eat a fucking cupcake without guilt?

According to the discharge notes, my case looked like a success on paper:

- Hospitalization: March 24, 1981 – June 22, 1981
- Height: 5'11"
- Weight @ admission: 101 lbs.
- Lowest Weight: 96 lbs.
- Weight @ discharge: 112 lbs.
- Vitals: All normal throughout, except low blood pressure @ 80/48
- Condition on discharge: Improved
- Limitations on diet: None
- Limitations on activity: None
- Medication: Elavil, 25 mgs. @ 8am and 75 mgs. @ 8pm
- Final Diagnosis: Eating disorder, probably Anorexia Nervosa associated with depressive feature.
- Case closed: December 24, 1981

"On the MHU, she had psychological testing, which also confirmed the diagnosis of Anorexia. The patient throughout her hospital stay indicated some dissension with her mother. She had a great deal of conflict about wanting to eat and yet being afraid to eat and gain weight. She admitted having considerable guilt when she did eat. During her hospital stay, she felt badly because she felt that she was sort of out of the picture at home and that her family went on living their lives and her illness did not seem to have much impact on them. Her mother tended to blame her weight loss on her exercising, but the patient did not exercise compulsively. She never did any self-induced vomiting.

"With the Elavil, the patient was able to admit that her spirits improved. The patient had mixed feelings about her discharge. She wanted to go home, but was afraid to go home. She was put on a modified behavior modification program, passes and home visits and eventual discharge were tied in with her weight gain. She was reluctant to accept the fact that her body image was distorted from her standpoint, but eventually she was able to accept the fact that she needed some external direction in regard to her caloric intake since her appetite control center was nonfunctioning with her present illness. She did complain of a lack of energy. At times she felt that she ate better when the nurses sat with her, but at other times she resented the fact that they did sit with her. She stated that she felt better when she lost weight in the hospital on occasion, because then she would be able to eat more. She stated that often she was able to eat more at bedtime because then she could fall asleep and not feel so guilty. She indicated that at times she felt like she was a failure because she gained weight and she felt successful when she was able to lose weight. She was somewhat fearful that when she eventually did leave the hospital, she would have difficulty maintaining her weight. She felt that guilt was one of the strongest feelings that kept her from gaining weight.

"Toward the end of her hospital stay, she indicated that she no longer felt proud when she did not eat. However, the nurses noted that even though she was eating more, she tended to stick to "diet foods". When she did begin to gain weight and was over 100 lbs. at times, she would become somewhat angry. At 108 lbs., she indicated that she was 'feeling fat.' She was told that she could be discharged if she were able to maintain a weight of 112 lbs. for a period of time. When it was felt that she had done this, she was discharged to be followed at the adolescent outpatient service of the MHU."

I included the discharge notes for the following reasons:

- The course of therapy I received in 1981 was successful in that I did not relapse after discharge - at least not enough to require hospitalization. That said, working to have a normal relationship with food after having Anorexia is not easy. Even if we take Anorexia out of the equation, every person's relationship with food is unique. Whether it's normal or not is a very subjective issue. Unlike a recovering alcoholic or drug addict that never touches drugs or alcohol again, an anorexic has to deal with food, and learn how to incorporate it back into his/her life in a healthy manner. We have to *re-learn* how to eat.
- Recognizing the comorbidities of depression and OCD in my case helped my recovery enormously.
- The complexity of the AN crazy, as reflected in my comments throughout the discharge notes.
- That others with Anorexia can learn what worked for me, as a reference point.

In a nutshell, it's never easy, not at any point in the recovery process. There's no eureka moment where you say, "Yes, I've recovered! I'm normal again!" Oh no. It doesn't work that way, at least for me. It is a slow, hard slog through the emotional, physical and spiritual equivalent of quicksand. Two steps forward, three steps back most days. Then, on other days, there's the light bulb moment that makes up for the hard times. It's the cumulative progress over time that truly counts.

As mentioned previously, I thought a lot about death throughout the whole AN saga. At some point, obviously, I decided (whether consciously or unconsciously) I didn't want to die from this illness. I didn't want to cash it in before I had even gotten started. I decided to become brave and be responsible and accountable for my own life.

Let's not forget the emotions. To be honest, I had mixed feelings when it came time to check out of the hospital and go home. The emotions were:

- *Fear!*

...of gaining too much weight
...of not being able to "make it" in the real world
...of not being accepted either at home with my family, or at school with my peers

- Excitement
- Doubt
- Loneliness
- Trepidation
- Frustration
- Regret
- Hopelessness
- Embarrassment
- Relief

Once I got home, I cried a lot during the months of July and August 1981. I was alone in my room in the proverbial forest of my thoughts. My social calendar was non-existent; after three months away I was detached from everything. It was a hard time; getting through the day without my AN rituals seemed overwhelming. I was learning to deal with my emotions vs. stuffing them down and pivoting to the false sense of control via food rituals.

As hard as it was, it was time to find a new way to live, eat, and become me. I had to figure out who I was without the Anorexia. I couldn't go back to living Anorexia, but I also couldn't go back to the way I was before Anorexia. I was 14 years old when it all started, and now I was 16 years old. A changed person. There was no going back.

The best way I could deal with getting discharged was to try and put it all behind me. Try to forget it ever happened to me. Why? Because it was such a dark time in my young life, and I felt some shame and embarrassment, mainly because of my parents. They didn't understand Anorexia, nor did they try. It was all about how much money my hospitalization had cost and the tension my treatment created between my mother and father. They didn't know how to deal with me, and so, as usual, they berated me and made me feel like it was all my fault. Like I was a burden. Like I was causing big problems. Like I needed to get it together, and be the model kid, whatever that means.

I spent the rest of the summer learning how to integrate back into the real world, putting weight on, and going to outpatient appointments with a counselor named Carol. The outpatient program consisted of twelve appointments through the months of July and August. I went to see Carol by myself, and kept ten of the twelve sessions. I told Carol my parents didn't want to be involved in my outpatient counseling. There was still conflict at home between Sly and Marty about how to deal with me, so they chose not to participate in the sessions with Carol. It absolutely did not help my recovery, because the tension was there. However, I could not control their behavior or choices, but I could work on trying not to feel guilty about it. The outpatient sessions weren't especially noteworthy. I think it was just part of the process, so that all the "I's" were dotted, all the "T's" were crossed, and my medical file could be closed.

Discharge notes concluded:

"....she was discharged to be followed at the adolescent outpatient service of the MHU."

The benefits of outpatient services are a bit murky. Carol evaluated me and noted:

"A month after returning home, Michele continued to experience depressed moods, concern about her gaining weight and at times still feeling fat. She also appeared to continue to be withdrawn with little involvement with friends as previous to her admission."

Okay, true enough. However, it's hard to just jump back into life in a month's time, after eight months of starving myself and then three months in the hospital. It's not a "pick up where I left off" simple solution. Obviously going back to starvation for me was not an option, although many sufferers of Anorexia do relapse. It's incredibly hard to reinvent yourself, especially at 16 years old! It's hard to find a healthy alternative for the patterns that anorexics get trapped in. I feel their pain, genuinely and acutely.

So, all through July and August 1981, I tried to re-enter my life. I couldn't go back to the weird food rituals to comfort myself; I had to learn to deal with my emotions, particularly anxiety, in some other way. Which is why, again, recovery is so very hard. I suppose it's like with any addiction or unhealthy behavior. Something has to replace it, or you'll relapse right back into the same destructive patterns. Yes, it's my hell, but familiar and therefore comforting.

I spent a lot of time by myself over those two months. I've always been comfortable being by myself. I enjoy the peaceful solitude. It's calming and soothing. Plus, I learned from a very young age how to occupy myself. There's nothing wrong with creating your own little bubble away from the rest of the world; it can be very healing. And it was healing. I was getting my mind right before going back to school in the fall. Looking up old friends, and trying to make new ones. Still, I'm not a loner. It's just about finding a good balance.

I had to create a new way of being for myself, post-AN. The seeds of AN had been planted when I was 14, so here I was, two-and-a-half years later on the other side of it. That's a big timespan for an adolescent. The remainder of the summer of 1981 was a lonely, hard time for me. I had taken myself out of the social loop. I had to find a way to re-enter my life and the world. It would have been so much easier if I had a cell phone to get lost in! No one was lining up outside my door to hang out with me. I'm sure many of my friends were uncomfortable and therefore unsure how to be around me. I don't blame them. If I had been them, I would have felt the same way. They saw how my outward appearance changed, and it must have been shocking. Who knows what they were told about me?

I had my friend, Doug, from 10th grade art class, who was sweet to me. He visited me in the hospital one time. When I got out, he invited me over to his house for an afternoon of TV watching and some serious snacking. On the coffee table in the living room, he had set out about a dozen bowls. Each bowl was filled with a different kind of snack. Sweet. Salty. Buttery. Crunchy. Chewy. Chocolatey. All of the bowls were carefully arranged to show the variety. They covered every inch of the coffee table. There were also small plates and napkins.

I don't remember what we watched on TV, but his thoughtfulness really touched me. I had a hard time "allowing" myself to snack, but I tried really hard, because he had made such a thoughtful effort. Doug made zero comments about what I ate. No pressure. No judgment. He did make a point of snacking, and showing his absolute enjoyment in doing so. I watched him. Doug was tall and slim, yet he was consuming handfuls of high calorie snacks. *He. Was. Having. Fun. And. Enjoying. Food.* He wasn't over the top with it. He ate what he liked and stopped when he was full, just like Kate on the day we did the bakery outing. She ate the cupcake, enjoyed the experience, threw the bag away, licked her fingers, and was done.

Again, for me, this was fascinating. I wanted to be like them so badly. But it was still too soon for me to know what "normal" looked like for me. I knew I had gotten all the external help I was going to get. And believe me, I was lucky to get the help. So now it had to be me; no one else was going to do it for me. Thus, the lonely, hard, state of mind I was in that summer. Anorexia is a lonely experience before, during and after however long the before, during, and after takes. For some, it can take years.

Doug was kind, patient, and generous in the best possible way. He wanted me to get well, but he wasn't pushy. He didn't understand the illness, but he cared about me and tried to focus on the positive. He was smart enough to know that being a good example was the best way to help me. He was right; the examples that people gave me of how to enjoy food in a healthy way were powerful elements in my recovery. Yes, Doug, was a bright spot in that summer of my 16th year.

As the summer drew to a close, I was scared. I was out in the big world with no restrictions. No 24/7 lockdown. No one constantly watching me. Going back out into the real world felt too risky. One false step, and catastrophe. There was also the danger of putting too much pressure on myself. Setting the bar too high. Perfectionistic tendencies were part of what got me in trouble in the first place. Nevertheless, school would be starting soon, and I had to be ready, or at least fake it until I made it.

It was time to find out what I was made of. Time to dig deep, and get strong. There was no reference manual on how to move forward after Anorexia. There weren't any books I could read about people who'd recovered, at least not that I was aware of. Believe me, I looked. There wasn't anyone like me that I could talk to. If there had been, I would have had questions, in addition to the ones listed at the beginning of this chapter.

- What are the pitfalls?
- What worked for you?
- What didn't?
- Did you have confidence that you'd make it?
- What did you tell people about your "time away?"
- If you relapsed, what did you do to get back on track?
- What did you do on days when depression (or OCD) took over?
- How did it change you?

All of these things to consider that I wasn't prepared for. At all. Extremely challenging, but not impossible. Or so I thought.

Fortunately, I had gained strength and worked hard to push all the negative feelings aside. Leaving the hospital was just the beginning of my recovery. It was interesting that Dr. G listed my condition at discharge as "improved." This was true, purely from the standpoint of weight gain. My victory was over the life-threatening stage of Anorexia, but my head was still a mess. The path ahead would be hard. I had to step up and take charge.

ME: "Hey, monster bitch, I'm putting you in a lockbox in the back of my brain, and that's where you'll stay. If you are indeed part of my DNA, I understand you'll never go away permanently, but I will keep you locked up, and throw away the key. You're done wreaking havoc. I'm leaving anorexic hell."

AN: "Oh no, you're not. You may have won this round, but you underestimate me."

ME: *"Oh yes, I am. Don't try to intimidate; it won't work. I know what you are now. You're a fucking monster bitch robbing me of my life. I know getting better is hard. Every day counts. I know you will try to insinuate yourself back into my thought processes. You're sneaky. Bring it on bitch; I'm finally ready to take you down."*

AN: *"You think you can get rid of me that easily?"*

ME: *"You're done. I won."*

AN: *"You just wait, girlie, you'll see."*

For the hard road ahead, I can say this. Find someone who you trust, and who you can totally be yourself with. Someone who accepts you without judgment. Like my grandma accepted me. There is someone out there just waiting to help you. Guaranteed. And it doesn't have to be someone you know. Look at organizations like ANAD.org, your local gym, church, school, neighbors. Chances are that people in these places know someone with an eating disorder.

When it comes to survival of Anorexia, everyone is different. There may be no relapses, or it may be a constant battle. At the very least, you'll never think about food the same way every again. And that's okay. You're stronger now, and you can handle this.

I was lucky enough to be part of the estimated 80% or so that survive this dreadful illness. In the fall of 1982, I went back to school and entered my junior year of high school.

Interestingly, when I tried going back to commercial art on that first day of 11th grade, it didn't work. I did all the right things. I headed to art class right after homeroom on the first day, feeling somewhat confident. I took a seat in front of an easel. Guess what? I could not sit in art class. I started to panic. Why? There was now a negative association between AN and art. I remembered sitting there the previous year and trying to draw or paint while the overwhelming, gnawing hunger in my stomach broke my concentration. Being cold constantly. I just couldn't do it. Art class put me right back in the nightmare. I didn't expect it. I felt that going back to art might jeopardize my recovery. As much as I liked being creative, I needed a fresh start.

Light Bulb Moment (#8)
AN kills passion and joy.

Ever since I was able to pick up a pencil, I loved to draw and do artwork. As a kid, I always looked forward to getting the paint-by-number set at Christmas. The historical museum in our city even had free art classes for kids on Saturday mornings. I looked forward to it every week. I loved the smell of the paints. I loved new brushes. Even today, going into a craft or art supply store, I get excited looking at all the art supplies; the colors, the fresh white sheets of paper and canvas, the quality of all the tools. The sheer number and variety of all the art tools. However, neither Sly nor Marty encouraged my artistic talent. In fact, one day when I was around seven years old, I was drawing a picture of a mouse. Sly looked at it and said, "You're not very good." And of course, her critique stuck in my mind. I wasn't good, and so I should never think of myself as an artist. Both Sly and Marty advised me that art was not something I should pursue, as I wouldn't be able to make any money. Better to do something practical, like business. This must have been playing out in my brain subconsciously, along the lines of, *Well, I've caused my family a lot of hardship by being sick with Anorexia, so now I should be the good daughter, and do something that I know they would approve of. I owe it to them for all the trouble I've caused.*

AN stole my love of art. I went to the principal's office and said, "I need to change my shop."

I switched to the business shop. The next day I went to the room with all the typewriters to learn typing, accounting and shorthand (yes, they still taught shorthand in 1982, which I actually used in college. It came in handy for the professors who spoke quickly during their lectures).

This should have been the end of the it, but no. When I sat down in the business room, I panicked again, and thought, *What am I doing here? I love art, don't I?* It was all so confusing. I didn't feel like I belonged anywhere. I probably would have done better just sticking to academics at a traditional school, but that wasn't an option at the burnout school. Bottom line, I flipped back and forth between art and business a few more times, and finally stayed in business. My re-integration was rocky; maybe I was taking it all too seriously. The school staff were very accommodating and patient.

It's hard to say what would have happened had I stayed in art. Would I have gotten an art scholarship for college? Would I have ended up with a more creative career than the business route that I chose? The bottom line is, it doesn't matter. At the time I felt giving up art was a small price to pay for getting well. Recovering was the most important thing. If art had to fall by the wayside, then so be it. Just because I didn't choose art at 17 years old didn't mean I couldn't choose it later. And I would.

In addition, there was the added stress of trying to assimilate back into high school life after being out for half of my sophomore year. How would the other students treat me? Would they think I was weird? The kids in commercial art seemed happy that I was back, especially Doug. I felt like I was betraying him by leaving, but I just couldn't be in art anymore; too many bad memories.

When I finally decided to stay in business shop, I made friends with Tracey and Lisa. We became the three amigos, and did everything together, both in and out of school. We laughed all the time. They never asked me about why I was out. They may not have known since I wasn't in their shop in 10th grade. Either way, it was a relief. I felt like I was getting a fresh start. I also felt like I was finally getting to enjoy the things teenagers did. This is what I was thinking about the day I went outside and played frisbee at the MHU. Getting off the sidelines, making friends. Having fun. Having a life.

CHAPTER 23
AFTERMATH

The staff members at MHU were extremely patient, and if not for them I don't know if I would have recovered as quickly as I did. Let me be very clear here. I absolutely needed outside help, otherwise I would not have made it. I would have become a statistic in the mortality category. It didn't matter where the help came from. It didn't matter that the treatment wasn't specially designed for Anorexia. My family and friends were not sufficient help. I needed the big guns - the health care professionals even though they were strangers. It was difficult at times to let these strangers see my vulnerabilities and weaknesses, not to mention the weird food rituals. But it was essential for them to see my illness in all of its ugliness before they could help me.

There is no such thing as a typical recovery for Anorexia. Each person is different and his/her path to recovery depends on the individual. Recovery could be compared to alcoholism. There are life events that can trigger unhealthy eating behaviors. The residue of Anorexia can last a lifetime. You're never the same after. It changes you.

The more I recognized that I had to toughen up and become the annihilator of this vicious illness, the more it helped my motivation:

ME: "If I can beat Anorexia, I can survive anything."

AN: "You're delusional, and you're living in a fantasy world."

ME: "You don't like my strong thoughts, do you AN? Too bad, bitch."

And so, I got on with my life. I felt better, not just physically, but I felt better about myself. Specifically, my self-esteem. I didn't want to relapse, because I deserved the full life that stretched out ahead of me even though I knew there would be many obstacles.

One of the first obstacles I faced was getting kicked out of the house in my freshman year of college. The year was 1984 and I was 19 years old. I wanted to take a trip to California over summer break to visit a friend who had grown up in Erie and was now living on the West Coast. I had saved enough money for the plane ticket and was planning on spending three weeks of the summer out in California, before starting my sophomore year.

On the topic of the trip, this was how the conversation went between Sly and me:

Me: I'm going to California this summer. I have $300.00 saved for the airfare, so I don't need any money from you or dad.

Sly: No, you're not going. I forbid it.

Me. Why?

Sly: You're not going.

Me. Yes, I am.

Sly: Well, if you insist on going, you are to leave this house and take all of your things with you before you go.

Me. Okay, fine.

And that was how I got booted out of the house in the summer of 1984.

Can you believe that? You would think Sly would enjoy having me out of the house for three weeks during the summer. When we were little, she would push us out the back door with a big bowl, saying, "Go pick some berries in the woods, and don't come home until suppertime." Then she'd lock the door!

I thought going to California was a great idea. I'd get to see my friend and I'd be out of her hair - a win-win. At nineteen, I was also tired of the dynamic with Sly. I needed to:

- Get away from the negativity
- Not be under her thumb anymore
- Find my identity

I moved out. I found an apartment with a roommate on East 13th street. The area was unofficially known as part of "the hood" in Erie. It was a bad neighborhood with all of the requisite drugs, crime, and violence.

I went to California, had a great time, and returned to the apartment. I had no car, and would have to use public transportation (i.e. the city bus) for work and school. I didn't care. I knew in the back of my mind this was going to be tough, but I had made my decision, and I didn't care.

One day I came home to find my roommate having sex with a guy in her bedroom with the door wide open. They made no effort to be discreet when they saw I was there; it was so uncomfortable. The apartment only had one bedroom, which my roommate already occupied before I got there. I had to put my bed in the living room, which was awkward, as it gave me no privacy. I turned around and walked back out the door. I'd rather go walking in the hood than have to look at them having sex.

Grandma heard I had moved to the hood. She knew what East 13th street was all about. She called me up and said, "You will come live with me." And that is why I was at Grandma's house when La-La moved in for hospice. With that simple statement, my grandma *saved* me, just like Dr. D saved me when he insisted Sly take me to the hospital. If it weren't for Dr. D and Grandma, I wouldn't be here today. There's no way I would have survived Anorexia without the both of them stepping in.

Grandma saved me in every way you can think of. Physically, emotionally, spiritually. I ended up living with her for five years before moving to Florida in 1988. Living with Grandma became a glorious extension of those weekends spent at her house when I was a kid. Whatever successes I've had in life are due, in large part, to Grandma. She was a force to be reckoned with. She was six-feet tall and wore a size twelve shoe. She bought men's sneakers to wear with her house dresses because she couldn't find women's shoes big enough. My tallness came from her, no doubt.

Getting kicked out of the house ended up being the best thing that had happened to me. Why? Grandma showed me what love was. She had three sons, and had always wanted a daughter. I was so lucky and privileged to have this woman as my Grandma.

During those five years, Grandma told me stories. In regard to Sly, she was not a fan. On top of not being allowed to hug us or show affection, Grandma continued, "The only time Sly ever hugged me was when I gave her an onyx ring that she really wanted." Otherwise, nothing, even after Grandma took her in when she showed up homeless on her doorstep after running away from Tulsa. Mind you, Grandma never had a bad word to say about *anyone*. It was not in her DNA to gossip or complain about others.

Grandma's stories were important to validate my questioning of my mother's behavior. Something was definitely "off" with Sly, and it wasn't just me; Grandma saw it too.

I was able to finish college living under her roof. I moved to Florida with a "mistake husband." I didn't have enough confidence yet or the funds to go on my own. My plan was to take my boyfriend. We'd go down there, and live together. If it didn't work out, oh well. However, my boyfriend insisted we get married first. Okay, why not? No money, no parental support, seemed like my only option. Bad choice, bad decision. It lasted all of four years. Why was it a mistake? He was verbally and physically abusive. This was something I knew about. When Marty was in his 30s, he liked to drink. A lot. He would hit the bar on the way home from work and drink for hours, then come home and hit Sly. He'd stumble home at midnight or so. This was before Sly got her waitress job. Maybe it was part of her reason to get the job so she didn't have to be home to deal with him at that hour. Marty was a mean drunk; when he came home after drinking all night he was loud, obnoxious and violent. It was a big reason why the quiet felt so weird to me at the hospital. Much of Marty's violence came from his biological father, who Grandma divorced when Marty was two years old. Imagine that. Marty's dad, Alexander, must have been very bad news for Grandma to get a divorce in 1942 in a town that was predominantly Catholic. It simply wasn't done. Wives back then just tolerated violence as part of being married. I never met Alexander, but I know he robbed a store and ended up in jail. He was abusive toward Grandma. So, Alexander was bad news, and when Marty drank, some of the bad he got from his dad surfaced.

Yes, Marty would hit Sly. They had knock-down, drag out fights that went into the wee hours. They were so loud there was no way my brothers and I could sleep through it, so we just lay in our beds, and wished it would stop. I was afraid to move. This violence was our norm; it was a big part of my childhood.

At 23 years of age, my frame of reference for a marriage included violence. However, when it happened to me, I dealt with it differently. Right after our wedding, he took the palm of his hand and slammed it into my head. I don't even remember what the conversation was about, but I remember thinking, *"Yep, here we go."* We had arrived in Orlando, FL and were staying with my new brother-in-law and his wife. They graciously let us stay in their home for a month, although the wife wanted us gone after a couple of days. We found an apartment, then a year later bought a home in Winter Springs, which is part of Orlando. Looking back, I'm surprised it even lasted four years. It might have been that our time at home didn't overlap much. Having completed my college degree, I worked a variety of desk jobs over the next couple of years. He worked retail, mainly evenings. He was a classic underachiever. And he lived for hunting, which was a big yawn for me. Once we moved into the house, he would invite hunting friends over to watch hunting videos. These were mainly hours of people sitting in trees in their camo with their guns waiting for an animal to appear. I didn't get it.

One night, we had a particularly vicious argument. We were in the kitchen. He took a golf club and starting breaking dishes with it. I ran into the bathroom and grabbed his electric razor. I opened the sliding glass door to the back yard and threw out the razor. We had a greenbelt behind us, so it went into the woods. He was so mad, he pushed me hard into the living room wall. I fell down on the floor. He picked me up, and dragged me out of the front door. Then he shut the door and locked it, so I couldn't get back in. Fun times, right? I ended up getting in through a window.

That was the turning point. My inner annihilator said, *Enough.* My husband had been planning a week-long trip back to Erie, PA, to go hunting. The next evening, when I came home from work, he was in the kitchen. I said, "You have two choices. You can either stay here and go to counseling with me or you can go on your trip. If you go on your trip, I won't be here when you get back. I will watch the house and take care of things while you're gone, but I will not be here when you return. Think seriously about what you want to do; it's your choice."

He didn't think I was serious, and he went on his trip. Upon his return, he was surprised to see the empty closet. He thought I was bluffing. No, not when you throw me against the wall, dude. I had to rid myself of this person and what he represented – kind of like another piece of Erie that I associated with Anorexia – commercial art, mistake husband, Sly. I had to remove every association. A simple divorce, and I could get on with it. I was 27 years old.

Back to the aftermath of AN; does anyone really recover? Hard to say since Anorexia is such a complex illness. As a survivor, I don't look like a skeleton anymore, but there is the residue of Anorexia that I carry with me throughout my life. The *potential* of weird behaviors, destructive rituals, repetitive OCD thoughts. Those things become more ingrained the longer the person suffers from Anorexia. There needs to be constant awareness, particularly if there is indeed a genetic component to the illness.

Speaking of skeletons and food, one day in 2020, I was in the grocery store and saw a young woman who looked like a walking skeleton, literally. She was wearing black spandex pants and a black top. Her legs were so thin I could have put my hands around her thigh and my fingertips would have easily touched each other with room to spare. I was afraid for her. My heart went out to her. I couldn't help but stare; it was that bad. No one who eats normally looks like that. No one who looks like that ever smiles either.

She was alone. I noticed another woman staring at her too. Our eyes met. The other woman just shook her head, and said to me, "That is so sad." The skeleton girl was nothing but skin and bones, no exaggeration. I wondered how she even had the energy to walk through the store. I frequented this store often, but never saw her again.

And I wondered, *Did I look like that at my lowest point of 96 lbs. on a 5'11" frame?* I don't know. I don't have any pictures of myself then. But if yes, it's no wonder Dr. D sent me to the hospital immediately.

I wanted to walk up to the skeleton girl and say, "I know what you're going through," but I wasn't brave enough. I don't know if it would have done any good. I don't know if it was appropriate. When you're at the stage of AN where you look like a walking skeleton, hearing words of concern from a stranger won't do anything. I probably would have made her mad. Again, there is resistance, because calling out an Anorexic on his/her Anorexia is fucking with their control. The words aren't powerful enough to penetrate the illness. They won't sink in.

The woman needed to be hospitalized with a nutrition IV. Even then people don't always recover. It is such an insidious, complex illness, which is why the mortality rate is so high. We loathe to give it up once AN sinks its claws into us.

The umbrella known as eating disorders (EDs) are a cross that millions of woman and men bear. Even Elton John admitted in his autobiography, *ME*, he struggled with bulimia. It was at the height of his rock star fame in the 1970s-1980s. Here was a man who had everything (like Karen Carpenter) and he still struggled with consuming large quantities of food then jumping up and down, so he would throw it all back up. Eating disorders aren't selective; they'll prey upon all, especially young people, who are still developing their sense of self-worth and identity.

In a perfect world, we'd look at food as simply the fuel we need to operate and to supply us with the energy to keep up healthy and our bodies running efficiently. We would eat when we're hungry and stop when we're full like a child does. When we're hungry, we would practice intuitive eating and always be in tune with what our body needs, in the right mix of nutrients and portion sizes. We would honor our cravings, whether it's an apple with peanut butter, or the mighty cupcake with loads of buttercream frosting. We'd naturally practice moderation every minute of every day. We'd feel gloriously spectacular all the time. Some people can do this. I admire them. Magazine and online articles tell us in greater detail how to be like these people. If we practice intuitive eating, we'll never have to worry about weight gain or loss. We'd feed our body what it needs and our weight would stabilize in a healthy range.

The world isn't perfect. We may read these articles and aspire to achieve food normalcy. But the truth is we know that on the day-to-day basis in the real world, most people struggle with food issues. I wish I could go back to the mindset I had when I was a kid: do my stuff, get hungry, have breakfast - lunch - dinner - snacks, and then get back to the joy of doing my stuff.

Since the world isn't perfect, let's be smart. Let's be vigilant. Let outside influencers such as publications, social media, celebrities, models and family be what they are. And we will be what we are. Let no external stimulus influence us in a negative way. Let's be strong and chart our own course with food, weight, and body image. Let's provide positive reinforcement instead of criticism. Let there be no comparison or judgment over who's the thinnest, most beautiful, or popular. As hard as it is in today's world, it's critical to focus on positive influencers and avoid the negative ones.

I still think about the skeleton girl in the store from time to time and I hope someone got her help before it was too late.

CHAPTER 24
BECOMING AN ADULT

I went into intense psychotherapy when I turned 30 years old. It was time to deal with the baggage I was carrying around from Sly and Marty once and for all. Sly for her ignorant cruelty. Marty for ignoring the problem. It was time for me to acknowledge that I was going to succeed in life not because of, but in spite of, my parents. By this time, I had walked my life path alone often enough to know I could do it, but I needed professional help. I needed an objective third party to tell me I was worthy of any and all good that came my way. I wanted the tools to look at myself at a higher level, and make the good happen. This is a big piece of anorexic recovery that often gets overlooked. It's great to get the number on the scale high enough to get out of the hospital, but gaining weight doesn't auto-matically mean 100% recovery. If recovery is the summit at the top of the mountain, I was still somewhere halfway up. Still climbing. Still trying to make it. My mountain was extra high and steep because my family was not supportive. At this point I could at least pat myself on the back for knowing I needed a therapist. I knew I could get to the top of the mountain, but I would need help, and it would be hard.

Why was counseling so important for me almost twenty years after Anorexia? I learned forgiveness.

Light Bulb Moment (#9)
Forgiveness is powerful and healing.

Learning forgiveness has made all the difference. Getting counseling when I was in the hospital at 16-years-old didn't mean I was good to go for the rest of my life. Three months of treatment for Anorexia wasn't necessarily going to fix the root problem(s). I needed to get further into adulthood, then go back and examine the problems that caused Anorexia in the first place. For example, the parental dysfunction. Was it still affecting me? Was it holding me back in any way?

Working through my stuff and learning how to practice forgiveness was hard. *Really* hard. A friend agreed to come with me on one session, so I could role play. The assignment was to pretend my friend was my mother. I had to tell her all the things she did to hurt me. By the end of the session, my friend's new white t-shirt was covered with my mascara smudges from all the crying and hugging I did with her. Gradually, I learned how to lose the destructive baggage. How to have better, more productive thoughts. Did it pay off? *Absolutely*. I had the tools to deal with the old childhood residue, was working on forgiveness, and could finally move forward. (More on this in the next chapter as it relates to Sly's Goodbye).

After my 30s and all the therapy, I moved from Florida to Texas. It was time to accelerate my career, which wasn't happening in Florida. Sometime during my 40th year, my emotions concerning my parents were starting to boil over and it was hard to keep a lid on them. The self-work was done, and the emotions had nowhere to go. I had to vent. I decided to write a heartfelt letter to my parents. Right, wrong, or somewhere in the massive gray area in between, I was finding my voice, and felt enough time had passed so I could address some things with Sly and Marty.

I did not keep a copy, but the gist of the letter was to let them know how much their lack of support hurt when I was going through Anorexia. I spent a lot of time and care with the letter. I was very careful not to blame them or play the victim. I reiterated several times in the letter that my intent was not to upset them, I just had to get this off my chest in order to move forward. Could they understand?

No, they could not.

I was having lunch at my desk at work and decided to check my personal emails. There was an email from Marty. The subject line read: "Your Letter." The email was just two sentences:

"We read your letter. Since this is how you feel about us, we will no longer be in your life."

What?

We will no longer be in your life?

Translation:

How dare you, Michele. We don't care what you think or feel. Since we have a giant size ego, we are now going to shut the door in your face. You're simply an extension of us, not a person in your own right. We cannot have a daughter that does not recognize us for the perfect parents we are.

As soon as I read Marty's email, I felt physically cold. Since I was at work, I went to find an empty office where I could shut the door and grapple with my emotions. I couldn't believe how callous and selfish they could be. Well, yes, I could.

Fast forward a couple months. I got a follow-up email from Marty:

Michele,

When I read your letter, I found myself somewhat angry. But, more than angry I was deeply hurt. Hurt to the point that I sat down and cried.

Being a parent is not the easiest thing in the world to be. From early on you make decisions, based, sometimes, on your own childhood experiences, that affect your child's life. I know this may sound like justification, but, I tried to do what was right for you. Sometimes no matter what you do it's the wrong thing.

One of my mistakes was not taking a more active role in your upbringing. That's not the only mistake I made, I'm sure.

My email to you was a first reaction to your letter, not a well thought out one. Since then I've done a lot of thinking and lost a lot of sleep over what to say to you.

If your mother and I didn't live up to your expectations as parents, it's not because we didn't try. We did the best we knew how to do. All we had to draw on was the way we were raised.

I'm sorry for the effects my mistakes have had on you over time and hope we can now get past all of this.

Let me end by wishing you a happy holiday season and saying that I love you.

Dad.

I thought, *Well, this is a start.*

Did they have verbally and physically abusive parents? Sly used to make me lie down on the bed on my stomach and take off my pants. She would drag her long nails along the back of my legs, looking for things to pop. It hurt like hell. Is this what her mother did to her? Or worse? I don't know, but at some point, as a human being, parent or not, there needs to be an understanding about how verbal and physical abuse damages the child. Sly hit me and Marty hit all three of us. Sometimes a belt was used. Shame on them. Neither was a saint in this regard. Just because it was done to you doesn't make it right. At least Marty tried to explain it in his note. He thought the parenting they were doing was the right way.

I wanted to get past all of it, too. I found out my brother Mark had a talk with them. He helped support them financially. I could be skeptical and wonder if they really sorry, or was their financial support in jeopardy unless they issued a retraction? I don't know and I didn't ask. I accomplished what I needed to, in that I got it off my chest. Their reaction was no big surprise.

Light Bulb Moment (#10)
There's a fine line between having a voice and showing respect for your parents.

By the age of 45, I had reached the pinnacle of my business career. All in all, a happy ending. A healing journey. Wait a minute, not so fast.

AN is like the beautiful, charismatic significant other you broke up with years ago. You're going along with your life. You're thinking, *I've got this figured out; it's working.* During these decades as a young adult, I basically buried AN in the back of my brain. I never thought about it or talked about it. I never joined any eating disorder organizations, or "told my story" until now. It was so bad, I just wanted to forget it ever happened. And I did, for a long time. I chose to keep it private.

Then one day, there's a knock on the door. You open it and there's AN, the charismatic, seductive force ready to take over your brain. You have a decision to make. You want to say yes. It would be so easy – slip back into the comfort of the AN rituals and destructive behaviors.

By the way, the knock could come when a significant life event happens. The emotions explode, and if they're not dealt with appropriately, the potential for relapse goes up proportionately. A job change, a bad break-up, money problems, illnesses, someone threw you under the bus. You saw a perfect body on TikTok and wonder why you can't look like that. Or you could, if only you ate less.

Here's a great example. In 2007 I ended a long-term relationship. I was 42 years old. It was heartbreaking, but it was the right thing to do. I did one of my major moves, from Texas to Ohio. About a year into the job, I talked with my boss about my job security there. The company was having some cash flow problems, however, the company had been in business since 1962. In rare instances when the company was in the red between the cash outlay for a project, and getting paid by the customer, the bank would always front a line of credit to bridge the gap. This was the situation when I said to my boss, "I'm thinking of buying a house. I know you can't guarantee my job, but how bad is this cash flow situation?" He said, "Don't worry, we have a line of credit; you're an integral part of the team, blah, blah, blah."

I bought the house, and six months later the company went under, another casualty of the 2008 recession. 2008 turned out to be a banner year; everything that could go wrong did. I was laid off from my job. A gang of thieves broke into my house one week after I moved in and stole my refrigerator and stove. They left the water hose to the ice maker on, which flooded my basement, kitchen, and dining room. My boyfriend broke up with me. A careless driver hit me and wrecked my car.

There I was, living the 2008 shit show in Ohio.

It would be easy to go right back into the AN-Depression-OCD nightmare. It was tempting. I was single. I lived alone. I felt the old familiar anxiety coming on strong. No one would see what I was doing. It would be so easy. Once you're an anorexic, you never forget how to do the tricks. I could start doing the freakiest food behaviors I could think of and no one would know. I could go back to spending an hour or two every night putting together a small bowl of granola to go with my tea, making sure it's just the right amount of cereal, no more, no less. Making sure the granola clusters chosen are "right" and putting them back in the cereal box if they're too large or too small to consume on any particular day. It would be like putting on my old, favorite bathrobe again, and getting under the three layers of blankets. Anorexia would be the perfect diversion. I wouldn't have to think about what to do next, or deal with the anger caused by a job loss. The fact that it happened *decades* ago didn't matter; a repeat is always possible.

The point is, there could be something in your life to trigger the old behaviors. The weird food rituals and restrictions. The thrill of seeing the number go down on the bathroom scale. Anorexia shows up and wants to draw you in. Say no to AN.

ME: "You're lethal. You're toxic. You made me look like a skeleton and you almost killed me. I know what you are. You're not charismatic. You're a monster bitch."

AN: "Remember all my good stuff, girl? It doesn't matter that you moved to Ohio, and got the rug pulled out from under you. I can put you back in control! I can distract you from ugly feelings! I can make you proud of yourself because I turned you into such a great

dieter back in 1980. You don't have to deal with life, just stop eating. It's easier. You know how, and you know you want to."

ME: *"No, I'm not going down this path again. AN, you can taunt me all you want. But you and I both know what you really are. Don't even try to glamorize. There will be no relapsing into your hell. No more psychological torment. No more damaging my body through self-imposed starvation. No."*

Consider these statistics on relapse and mortality:

- "Anorexia Nervosa is a devastating eating disorder with a mortality rate six times that expected for young women. Current behavioral and pharmacological treatments remain inadequate, with low rates of recovery and high rates of relapse." (Dr. Alexandra Muratore, www.national eatingdisorders.org, April 11, 2023).
- The highest risk for relapse from Anorexia Nervosa occurs in the first 18 months after treatment, with 35% falling back into eating disordered behaviors. (www.eatingrecoverycenter.com, extracted from a BMC Psychiatry Study, 2016)

Much of the research suggests there is a lack of structured programs to address relapse. All of which leads to the point I've been making all along. This is a serious illness. It's not just "she's not eating, she's just doing it for attention, she can stop whenever she wants."

Be strong when triggers happen. Understand that life happens. Understand that others don't understand. Know how Anorexia can always come back. If and when it does, slam the door shut. You do not have to be a relapse statistic. Get help to shut that door and keep it shut.

Every time I indulge in sweets, AN wants to come back. As mentioned, I love a good donut. Sometimes I hear Anorexia in the back of my brain screaming when I look at a donut. There is a bakery called Cinotti's in Florida. It has the *best* cream filled donuts (topped with chocolate). When I visit Cinotti's, there is always a line out the door. It is a family owned business since 1936, and customers are loyal; they're willing to wait in line for however long it takes to get their baked goodies. Whether Cinotti's, Jack Frost, or Colonial Bakery, going there and enjoying a donut with a good strong hot cup of coffee is symbolic. I slam the door in AN's face and eat the damn donut. I do my best to enjoy it. Sometimes the old thoughts will come in saying, *"Don't eat that,"* but I do my best. One donut (or cupcake) at a time.

CHAPTER 25
SLY'S GOODBYE

By now, you may think Sly is the villain in my story. Or is Anorexia the villain? Two monster bitches instead of just one. My life at 16 was a cruel monster bitch BOGO ("buy one, get one") event. Regardless, Sly was oblivious to the havoc she had wreaked in my life. Truth be told, I didn't want or need to disclose to her how much pain she caused me because I didn't want to give her the satisfaction. She wouldn't have understood anyway. Sly was a woman with major psychological problems, who didn't know how, or want, to be a mother. Even on her deathbed, in 2017, she never talked about how she treated me throughout my life. No remorse, apologies or regrets were ever offered.

I did not initiate the topic with her because:

- I had forgiven her, and,
- I wanted to respect her decision(s) on what to say or not say, as she prepared to leave this world.

It was June of 2017. I was 52 years old, and had moved from

Columbus, Ohio to Phoenix, Arizona. My soon-to-be husband, John, lived there. Giving up my gig in Ohio, and moving across the country was a leap of faith, but by this time I had grown into my confidence, and my inner annihilator kept me on the right track. I was leaving the library, and sitting in my car organizing things when my phone rang. It was the middle of the afternoon.

Marty: Your mother has been diagnosed with Stage 4 colon cancer.

Me: *What?* She's never been sick a day in her life!

This was true. Sly was 74 years old, and the only time she was ever in the hospital was when she was giving birth to three kids. However, Sly was experiencing an irregular heartbeat, or AFib (atrial fibrillation). It seems her body was under extreme duress from the cancer, and was stressing out her heart. The doctors had the diagnosis right away. Her lungs had spots on them and her liver was riddled with cancer.

Marty told me the Stage 4 diagnosis was basically a death sentence.

Colon cancer begins as a polyp and grows slowly over many years. Sly may have had the cancer for a long time and not known it. Or perhaps she knew something was wrong, and didn't say anything. I remember a phone conversation with her at Christmas time 2016. She mentioned she hadn't done any holiday baking because she didn't feel good. I thought that was a little odd because she loved to bake and never got sick. The cancer must have already been at the critical stage then, but she didn't do anything about it until her heart started acting up and forced her to deal with it. Again, speculation on my part. We kind of know when things are off in our body right?

Sly's cancer diagnosis brought up a lot of "stuff" for me psychologically. I wondered if Sly would come clean with me, although, honestly, I don't think she was capable. She was broken. I do not know her childhood story, only that there was some type of abuse in her background before she met Marty, which was why she wanted to get married so badly, so she could get out of the house. She cut herself off from her family permanently. She never, ever talked about her childhood. When I say she was broken, I think the abuse probably scarred her for life.

In July, I got another call from Mick. He still lived in Erie and was doing all the caregiver work for Sly – an exhausting job that he did outstandingly well. Mick said they were rushing Sly into surgery because her intestine was so poisoned that if they didn't take it out, she was going to die immediately. She made it through the surgery. They put a colostomy bag on her, which was permanent. She resigned herself to the fact that it was the end. After the diagnosis, she talked about doing chemotherapy and trying to beat it. If the chemo killed the cancer, she could go back to living a normal life. A big thing with her was she wanted to wear pants, because she liked to garden. With the colostomy bag, she wouldn't be able to do that. She also didn't want to live her life dealing with a permanent bag collecting all of her body's urine and bowel movements.

As an aside, her resignation to the diagnosis make sense to me. In 2016, I had met a spiritualist up in a town called Jerome, Arizona. I was there with some friends. We made a stop there on our way to Sedona, because Jerome is an old mining town with a lot of history around ghosts. People book there years in advance on Halloween so they can have a potential "ghost experience."

Out of the blue, the spiritualist, who I didn't even know, said to me, "Your mother is straddling both worlds." She explained further. "Her contract was done at 67 years old, and she wanted to leave then, but agreed to stay longer in order to take care of your father." In other words, 67 must have been the last of her five exit points, and there was a way to extend it. Sly may have even been at the point of no return in 2016 with the cancer. Again, given it was slow growing, she probably had it for years before the diagnosis. In hindsight, I guess I could understand this because in her later years Sly seemed kind of "checked out." She didn't enjoy taking care of Marty. He could be very difficult to deal with, and had a host of health problems. High blood pressure, diabetes, and a bad back, just to name a few. They still lived at home, so what would happen if Marty, who is 6′5″, fell over from sugar shock? There would be no way she could get him up. I think she was phoning it in, biding her time, and when the diagnosis was given, she accepted it and didn't fight back at all, at least from what Mick and I saw. He was with her most of the time, and said she never broke down.

At the end of August 2017, I made a trip back to Erie. Sly was in a very nice, assisted living community, in the critical care section. This center was just five minutes up the street from my parents' house. It had a long waiting list, but they were able to get her into a private room, because she had volunteered there for eighteen years with her friend Dorothy, and they wanted to return the favor. I was happy about this. Despite everything, she deserved comfort in her last days.

I wasn't sure what to expect when I got there. Didn't know what Stage 4 cancer would do to a person's appearance, energy level, or emotional state. Surprisingly, when I arrived in town, and got to the center, she looked good. In fact, she didn't even look sick. It was amazing. She had makeup on and seemed to have good energy. She was wearing a colorful nightgown with front snap closures that hid the colostomy bag well. It seemed like it was important to her to maintain her appearance during the last stage of her life, which would explain the effort made with the makeup and colorful clothes.

During my visit, Sly was on an antibiotic drip to fight infection. The doctors said she had anywhere from one to five years. I believed the doctors because she looked good. I thought I had the luxury of time to prepare for her death. In reality she only had three weeks left.

One day I was in Sly's room with Dorothy. Dorothy was trying hard to put up a cheerful front, but I could tell she was crying inside. The newspaper had arrived. On the front page was a story about an Erie woman who had passed away at the age of 111. I couldn't believe it! I started reading the story out loud to Sly and Dorothy. As part of the article, they interviewed the woman and of course asked the question, "How did you get to live to 111?" She said she had never been in the hospital, and supposed she would just die of old age at some point. She was happy to have lived a good life, and had no regrets. She also said she never had any children. Immediately Sly commented, in a scornful tone, "That's why she lived so long."

Through multiple times of questioning Marty, I finally confirmed that Sly never wanted children. I asked him point blank one time, "Did Sly have kids because you both wanted them, or did she have kids because if you were a woman in 1960 that's what you did?" He answered with the latter. She had three kids, didn't want kids, and felt trapped for the rest of her life. How's that for taking charge of and being responsible for yourself? As a result, you impacted three human beings in a profound way.

Light Bulb Moment (#11)
Sly didn't want kids.

Therefore, I'll never have the mother I wanted because my mother didn't want me. Nothing I can do about it. Learn to accept it.

Light Bulb Moment (#12)
Let my parent die in peace.

Letting my parent die in peace was a gift I could give her vs. trying to extract something she couldn't or wouldn't give. I could do this. It would be okay.

Light Bulb Moment (#13)
It's not my fault.

When I heard her comment on the 111-year-old, I actually felt sorry for her. What a waste. Yes, you had kids you didn't want, but you could have found ways to be happy in your life. If you were so miserable, you could have gotten a divorce, given custody to Marty, and moved on with what you really wanted to do. Maybe she didn't know what she really wanted, or even, worse, didn't care either way, so she stayed stuck. Sadly, fear of the great unknown keeps our dreams at bay even when we have a crystal-clear vision of what our dreams are.

Back to 2017. Obviously, this time was all about making Sly comfortable in her last days. Again, as Sly lived out her last few weeks, I wondered in the back of my mind if there would be any kind of reckoning or something in the way of an apology. There was not. I was not surprised.

I put much of my energy during those two weeks helping out at my parents' house. Marty was still at home. They lived in a very nice, two-story home with a finished basement. It was filthy; not a healthy place for them to live. Apparently, neither of them had cleaned the house in a long time. I took it upon myself to do a thorough top-to-bottom cleaning, which was beneficial for many reasons. It kept me busy, kept me distracted from my thoughts, and it needed to be done.

One day, I was cleaning the master bathroom and noticed the scale. I had on jeans and a t-shirt. I stepped on the scale. The digital reading said 138 lbs. This was twelve pounds below my normal weight. It was also a few pounds less than the 142 weight I had in 8th grade when the whole AN nightmare started. My first thought was, *Is there something wrong with the scale? There has to be.* At 52 years old and 5'11" tall, I had weighed 150 lbs. for the last fifteen years. How did I drop twelve pounds without noticing? Later in the day, I took Sly to a doctor's appointment at the hospital. While she was in the blood lab, I saw a weighted scale in the hallway just outside the room. I still had on the same clothes. The scale said 138. *Well, it must be right then; that's my weight.*

Then I became aware that the clothes I had on were loose. My thought track became, *Uh oh, what's going on here? Is the AN monster bitch back for an encore? Nonsense. Relapse doesn't happen forty years later. Does it?* I ignored the bitch during the 2008 Ohio shit show, so losing twelve pounds was no big deal. I decided, *It's not that important, given everything else that's going on.* I chose to ignore it. Once Sly's goodbye was finished, I'd gain it back. Rationalization and dismissal. End of self-talk.

I stayed in Erie for two weeks. During this time, as I was taking it all in, I honestly thought Sly might make it. On my last day in town, I asked Sly if she wanted to go outside and sit in the courtyard. She said yes, so I wheeled her out in the requisite wheelchair. I took her to the courtyard and parked her next to one of the benches. I put the brake on, and sat next to her on her left. It was a lovely, bright end of summer day. From the location of the assisted living facility, we had a great view of Lake Erie. Erie was indeed very pretty during the summer months.

Once she was settled and comfortable, Sly talked a little bit about doing some chemotherapy, which she had not done up to this point. She was inclined not to do it, but hadn't made a firm decision yet. She was still healing from the emergency surgery in July. She had an IV antibiotic to treat an infection in her abdominal area. Per the doctors, the infection had to be cleared up before she could start chemotherapy. A few days earlier, I had taken her to a check-up with the surgeon. When they lifted up her housecoat, I was aghast. Her whole midsection had been cut open. And the bag was attached to what was left of her intestine. It reminded me of soldiers that get blown up and their insides are falling out of their abdomen. The doctor cleaned it up and didn't appear to be concerned about the healing process. While the doctor was doing this, Sly said, "Thank you for saving my life." The doctor said, "That was God."

As Sly was talking on the bench on the last day of my visit, I turned to look at her full on. Outside, in the sunshine, it was obvious that her skin was turning yellow. I didn't see it inside, in the artificial lighting. Her liver was giving out. It was really noticeable. I thought, *Wow, she's turning yellow, but she still looks good.* I still had that one to five year life expectancy in my head, per what the doctors had advised.

I had taken her to another specialist who was monitoring the infection, and had, in fact, prescribed the IV drip. She took a blood sample from which she'd be able to determine the status of the infection. There was good news a couple days later when the specialist called me to say that the infection had cleared up and was completely gone. Sly could stop the IV and move ahead with the chemo if she so desired. Obviously, she had been thinking about it, because she said, "I have to let the doctor know if I want to start chemo. If I don't do the chemo, well I guess that's it." (Curiously, Marty would utter similar words two years later; see next chapter). She said it in a matter of fact way, but with a slight trace of sadness and resignation. That was the closest she got to showing emotion; at least when I was there. For a brief second, I saw the mask come down.

Also, as she sat there in the sun, I could see the beginning of the separation. It's been said that when you're at the end of this life, if you have the time to prepare, you start to become aware of the next thing. Some people see loved ones who have departed. Some experience a wonderful peace. Some even become happy because they know they're going home.

I didn't know that sitting outside in the courtyard with Sly during my last day in Erie would serve as our goodbye. Sometimes it's better not knowing it's the last time you'll see someone. If I had known it was the last time, I may have been more emotional – or said things she didn't want to hear – or worse yet, cried – none of which would have benefitted her in any way. Better to stay neutral and let two people enjoy an hour in a courtyard filled with flowers and sunshine.

After about a half-hour, I wheeled Sly back to her room. She was tired. It was time to leave and say goodbye. Two other family members were there in the room with me. We had all come from out of town and were getting ready to head to the airport. The three of us each gave her a hug, we said goodbye, and left. My other two family members were ahead of me. Once I left the room and was just outside her door, something told me to slow down. I looked back and was able to see Sly out of the corner of my eye, but she couldn't see me. She was sitting in bed, with her gaze fixed straight ahead. I didn't think it consciously, but something in that gaze told me, *She knows she doesn't have much longer.* It was the second time I saw her facade come down. There were no tears, just an expression that read, *I know that's the last time I'll see them.* She died on September 26, 2017.

The day of her death, I was back in Phoenix. I just felt off. It was the oddest thing. It was a Tuesday and I was preparing for another trip to Erie on Thursday, since Mick had informed me she was declining. I had errands to run, one of which was stopping by See's

Candy to pick up a couple of boxes of chocolates to take back to Erie. See's isn't available on the East Coast, so I always brought some with me. I was standing in the middle of the store, and started crying for no reason. I tried to be quiet about it, and I don't think anyone noticed. Again, my classic middle child behavior of going to great lengths to avoid making a scene.

Perhaps someone did notice. I composed myself and got in line. I made my selections, and got ready to pay the cashier. She added an extra box of candy to my order, but didn't charge me for it. She said, "The man ahead of you bought this for you." I said, "Wow, that is so nice." She said, "He comes in here often, and has been known to do this." Did he notice I was upset, and wanted to extend a kindness? Or maybe it was just random? I don't know, but the whole after-noon went the same way - crying intermittently, running into kind strangers, and doing my errands as best as I could, given my emotional state. In hindsight, I think the crying was beneficial. I got the emotions out before getting to Erie so I could remain composed, since my family rarely shows emotion.

I finished all the errands and arrived home in the early evening. I told John, "I just feel off, I'm going upstairs for a while." I ended up in the upstairs bathroom. I sat on the edge of the bathtub, and started crying hard. This was surprising, for two reasons:

- I thought I had gotten it all out earlier, and
- I had no clue as to why I was crying.

As I sat there crying by myself, I started getting this vision. I saw an army of angels marching. They were coming from the right. There were four rows of them. Each row was at least six angels deep. How did I know they were angels? Well, they looked like pictures I had seen in books, and on Catholic holy cards and such. White, with gigantic wings. The other thing I noticed was that these were big, strong, fierce angels. Soldier angels. Wow. They marched with purpose and precision. If you got into trouble, you would want these angels to have your back. I wondered, *Where are they going?* Then I knew. They are going to get Sly and bring her over. I was experiencing this at just after 6:00 pm Arizona time. I learned the next day that Sly died just after 9:00 pm East Coast time.

Once I got the news on Wednesday morning, I went to my favorite mountain for solitude to grieve and to process. Afterward I was fine and moved on. The grieving period for Sly was a day on the mountain in Phoenix.

A few months later, in early 2018, I had a vivid dream that helped explain her broken state during life. It was one of those lucid dreams that felt like it actually happened. The setting for this dream was Ft. Lauderdale, Florida. It was late afternoon. All five of my family members were outside having a picnic. We were at an outdoor park, sitting at a picnic table near the ocean. It was very quiet and peaceful in this space. Everyone was enjoying the picnic very much as the afternoon wore on.

Around twilight, Sly took me by the hand and said, "Let's go for a walk." We walked together on the sidewalk as night fell. We were heading to Miami. In the dream, there were only about four short city blocks between Ft. Lauderdale and Miami. I was looking down at the sidewalk, which had a lot of detail. I was watching my feet, because there were many cracks in the sidewalk, and I didn't want to trip and fall. I also was having a hard time keeping up with Sly. She was ahead of me and moving fast. Upon arriving in Miami, we came to a stretch of beach. The ocean was on the left, and a big event was set up on the sand right near the water. We were still a few blocks away. When I looked up, Sly was still ahead of me. She continued to walk very fast, with purpose like she knew exactly where she was going and what was up ahead. And other than,

"Let's go for a walk," she never said another word during the dream.

At this point, I was excited. I was doing something with my mother that she had initiated. She wanted to show me something. As we approached Miami, I saw it was a carnival. Lots of people, lights, carnival rides, and music. It looked and felt very festive. Colorful. Neon lights. It looked like carnival time in Brazil, or Mardi Gras in Louisiana.

All of a sudden, Sly went into the carnival and my two feet came to a dead *stop* right at the entrance. There was no demarcation line, but I knew with every cell in my being that I could not go in. I looked down at my feet. They were right behind an invisible line, and would go no further. A message came through loud and clear, "No, you don't go in. This is not for you."

I couldn't see Sly. She had disappeared in the carnival. I stepped back a few paces, and looked at the carnival again. On the water, there were dozens of very tall, brightly colored, super huge daisies. They were several stories tall. I thought it was weird that these gigantic flowers would be in the ocean, swaying gently back and forth. Again, they were very bright and there were a lot of them. As I continued to look at them, I got the feeling there was something sinister about them. As soon as the thought crossed my mind in the dream, they all turned toward me at the same time and looked right at me. Each daisy had a large *eyeball* in the center. My next thought was, *Oh, this is bad.* The whole carnival was a bad scene, and Sly was lost in there somewhere. My dream ended.

In my waking state, the flowers with the eyes had not faded from my memory at all. In fact, the dream gave me insight into perhaps what my mother had to endure. My theory is sexual abuse, of course. I suspect sexual abuse on a large scale. This was what she had to deal with growing up in her family, and was what caused her to divorce herself from them permanently. It was what broke her as a human being. I suspect no one in her family protected her, and more than likely pretended nothing was amiss. I don't have the facts, just brief conversations with Marty, who alluded to it...and the godawful dream. If they never acknowledged it, they poured salt in the emotional wound. Sly would have said, "I'm done with you hypocrites." She escaped by marrying Marty.

She never talked about the abuse. But based on those creepy eyeballs, it must have been bad. The dream, therefore, gave me answers about what was unspeakable. Even if she had wanted children, would she still have been incapable of giving love, affection and positive reinforcement? I also think this may have been part of her "work" after she passed over (i.e. you hurt Michele deeply. She is a beautiful soul, you need to try and explain. Do it in a dream). I believe if we hurt people in this life, either knowingly or unknowingly, we are accountable and need to make amends.

But wait, there's more on the whole sinister eyeball thing.

The counselor for my therapy sessions in my 30s was gifted. She was one of the few clinicians in Florida that was trained on music therapy. She would have me lie on the floor in her office in a comfortable position, with a blanket and pillow, or whatever else was needed. Once I was settled, she turned on classical music. She guided me through whatever images or thoughts manifested. The best way to describe it is to say it was like a lucid hypnosis. As such, it would encourage stuff in the subconscious to "manifest" and be dealt with should that stuff not serve my well-being.

On December 12, 1998, we began one of these sessions. As the music started, Lora (not her real name) said:

L: What are you aware of?

Me: Starting to think about the ocean. It is soothing, calming. It's helping me relax.

L: Take in the scene.

Me: I'm alone, moving in slow motion. There's a boat out there.

Someone is on the boat and he is looking at me with a telescope. Wonder why.

L: Stay with it.

Me: One big eyeball. It's magnified by the telescope. Like a distortion, weird.

L: How do you feel?

Me: It's really weird because I'm moving down the beach and the telescope is following me and getting longer. Eyeball at the end of the scope is getting bigger, and watching me. I don't like it. Creepy.

L: Ask. What does it want?

Me: It says, "You're not allowed here."

The large eyeball in this 1998 session was the same as the one from the dream I had about Sly and me at the sick, twisted beach carnival. The dream happened in 2018 a few months after Sly died – a full 20 years after the 1998 therapy.

They. Were. The. Same. Eyeballs.

Sinister. Freaky. Creepy.

And, in both scenarios, I was not allowed to be there.

I guess it's all symbolic of the sexual abuse. For me, it was one eyeball coming through a telescope. It represented my uncle. He liked to go after the girls. The younger, the better. When I was a young girl, he liked to get me alone and try to put his hand down my pants. He succeeded a few times. Then I told him to stay away from me. I did everything I could to stay away from him. He moved on to younger girls. Years later, he eventually went to prison for forcing his stepdaughter to perform oral sex on him while holding a gun to her head. A sick, perverted individual.

For Sly, if the eyeballs represented abuse, then instead of one like me, she had many. There were so many daisies out there in the ocean with their big eyeballs swaying.

Given all of this, she must have had a broken childhood, grown up to be a broken human being and was in no way fit to be a parent. Was being a non-mother her way of coping? Was she purposely being malicious? Was her mother verbally and physically abusive to her? I don't know, but I suspect yes. Where else would she get the horrific idea to pull my hair out? Or pour soap in my mouth because I sassed her? Or criticize her only daughter for starving herself? Or worst of all, withhold love? Maybe all those behaviors felt normal to her, based on her childhood. Sly hadn't a clue on how to deal with any aspect of being a parent, period. She was angry at me. How dare I play this starving game for attention? Don't expect me to be your mother. I never wanted you. I'm damaged goods.

Light Bulb Moment (#14)
Look at the big picture, and learn from it.

ME: If the mother magic had happened, Anorexia might have left me alone. I wouldn't have this opportunity to help others who are struggling with Anorexia. They might even be encouraged, because I've walked in their shoes, and I know what they are going through. I know how hard it is."

Always a silver lining, if one looks long enough.
Always something to learn, if one tries hard enough.

CHAPTER 26
MARTY'S PARTY

"Dad is in the hospital with pneumonia," Mick said. It was early August 2019.

Physically and psychologically, Marty had a tough time after Sly passed in 2017. We all thought he would be the one to go first, given his multiple health issues. In addition to the high blood pressure, diabetes, and a bad back, he had heart disease and gout. He had been a life-long smoker and was paying the price. I thought surely Marty would go before Sly. When that didn't happen, I figured he would follow after Sly quickly. I remember reading stories about how that was fairly common for spouses who had spent a lifetime together. When one died, the other went fast. Marty and Sly had been together over 57 years when she died.

Marty stuck around for another two years. His soul didn't want to leave, but his body was completely worn out. As opposed to Sly, whose soul had been ready to leave years before her body succumbed to cancer. It was a shock to him when she died. He simply couldn't wrap his brain around it.

On the day Sly died, Marty was in surgery. He had to have his right leg amputated up to the mid-thigh due to diabetes. Sly was at home under hospice care administered by Mick. She didn't think Marty would make it through the surgery, and was surprised when he did. She was very much awake and aware; when she passed in the evening, it happened quickly. Mick had to go to the hospital the next morning to give Marty the news.

Marty had survived a lot of close calls over the years. From open heart surgery to an eight-hour back surgery, he had always come out of it okay. Nevertheless, taking care of him was high maintenance, which Sly had done all on her own up to the point of her cancer diagnosis.

In the months following her death, it became obvious that Mick couldn't care for him at home any longer. In addition to mobility issues caused by the leg amputation, he also needed insulin shots in his stomach. He had trouble with hygiene tasks and going to the bathroom. His balance was poor. His blood sugar levels would spike and tank (he often snuck forbidden food), leaving him confused and dizzy.

Mentally, he was extremely stubborn and depressed. In short, he needed to be cared for by professional health care personnel. He needed to be in an assisted living facility where nurses could care for him 24/7. Luckily, he was admitted into the same facility where Sly had been.

However, he remained depressed. His perception was that he had lost his freedom. He wanted to be back home, and he wanted things to be as they were before Sly died. He simply didn't deal well with change. Even though the facility was one of the best around, he didn't like being there, not for one minute. And he let everyone know it constantly. He chose to dwell on what he didn't have vs. what he had. He was mad that Sly died first. A container of her ashes and a picture of her were displayed in his room; he looked at them and yelled, "You weren't supposed to go first – you really messed up!" He was mad that he couldn't drive anymore. He missed simple routine things; he couldn't go to McDonald's and get a coffee like the old days. He was mad about being in pain most of the time.

Over the course of the two years, he gradually gave up. Right after the amputation, he willingly went to physical therapy to learn how to walk with a prosthetic limb. He would often talk about coming out to Arizona to visit, once he got the hang of the leg, and felt strong enough. He talked about visiting, but he was too frail to do a cross country trip. A four to five hour flight would have been way too much. And what would we have done if something happened while he was with us? But the idea of coming out to visit made him happy, so we talked about it often.

I couldn't understand then why he gave up. In hindsight, though, his body was simply giving out. He stopped going to physical therapy. The prosthetic leg stayed propped against his bedroom wall, unused. He would sit in his room with the lights off, the curtains drawn, and do nothing.

There was one positive thing Marty did during this time. I usually called him once a week; he would always end our phone conversation with "I love you." He may have had regrets about wanting to express love and affection but not doing it because he wasn't raised to express his emotions – guys didn't do that. Regardless, when he first started doing it I was surprised, but grew accustomed to it quickly. It's never too late to tell people you love them.

Speaking of regrets, a couple years before either Sly or Marty were seriously ill, I was visiting them. Getting booted out of the house in the summer of 1984 event came up in conversation. I'm sure I'm the one that brought it up, probably just to see if there would be any remorse or apology.

Marty: I said you could stay (truth: he didn't).

Sly: I'm old fashioned.

What the hell does that mean? You don't approve of your 19-year old daughter going off to California for a summer vacation? Of seeing a world outside of Erie, PA? They just didn't get it, and that's okay. Since they were the parents, and I was the kid living under their roof, they had the right to kick me out if I was not honoring their wishes. Their wishes didn't need to make sense. They didn't need to have a good reason. The whole thing was lame.

In August of 2019, when I found out Marty was in the hospital with pneumonia, I thought the stubbornness would win out over the depression. It didn't seem like he was ready to leave yet, and was fighting it – the exact opposite of Sly's response to her mortality. I wasn't too concerned, because he had been in and out of the hospital multiple times over the previous two years. They fixed him up, sent him back to the nursing home, and all was well.

When I got to Erie on August 17th, Marty looked frail and weak. Turns out he had dysphagia, a condition that impairs the swallowing reflex. This morphed into aspiration pneumonia, a condition when food is breathed into the lungs instead of being swallowed into the esophagus and stomach. His lungs become infected. The course of treatment is antibiotics and an alternate way to take in food, such as a port or IV. Recovery depends a lot on how severe the pneumonia is, along with any other underlying health conditions.

It's a common condition in elderly people. The only option Marty had was a feeding tube, which could be permanently inserted in his stomach. He would never be able to enjoy a meal again. Ironically, eating was one of the few things left in his life that he could enjoy. He could have three squares a day plus snacks; all he had to do was place his order and go to the dining room. It was also an opportunity for Marty to socialize. He was more apt to engage with other residents as opposed to Sly, who stayed in her private room and took her meals there. He made a few friends at meal time. They would all sit at the same table. Now he couldn't even be able to do that anymore.

The doctors told Marty it was his decision whether or not to put the tube in. Initially, he said yes, because, again, his soul wanted to hang around. I don't think he was ready to go yet, even though he was depressed and didn't like where he was living. It's the old adage: "We're comfortable with what we know." In Marty's case, sitting in his dark room with depression and physical pain was more desirable than death (unlike Anorexia). The thing is, Marty had it pretty good in those two years after Sly died, but his perception was his reality.

Unfortunately, the pneumonia had progressed to the point where he was too weak for the procedure, and therefore, the doctors were hesitant to do it. It became a Catch 22. No food plus pneumonia made him too weak for the feeding tube, but he needed the tube to get nutrients to help get his strength back. It was the beginning of the end.

As I listened and observed everything, I couldn't see the finality of it all.

Marty's body was shutting down. But he was my dad; he couldn't leave yet! During the time I was there, all I could do was give him hydration. There was a cup filled with sponge sticks on the tray by his bed. The sponges, about the size of a sugar cube, were attached to the end of what looked like a large tooth pick. I soaked the sponge in lemon water and gave it to him to suck on – as much as he wanted. He was lucid and seemed to know what was going on. The doctors moved him to ICU because his vitals were deteriorating.

On Wednesday, August 21, I sat with him in the ICU. Several HCPs were in and around his room, along with Mick, my cousin Mary, and my husband John. Our flight back to Phoenix was out of Cleveland, departing in the late afternoon. We needed to allow enough time to drive from Erie to Cleveland to catch the flight. Time ran out quickly, and soon we had to leave. Mary said, "Say goodbye to your dad," and everyone left the room.

I thought, *Why is everyone being so serious? He's going to make it, he always does.* She got it and I didn't. My brain wouldn't accept it. I sat down on the bed and got my face close, so Marty could focus and understand that I was leaving. My face was only a few inches from his.

When his eyes met mine, I could see the separation already taking place. I saw it with Sly, and now here it was again. I could see his soul coming through behind his eyes. His soul, whether willing or unwilling, was getting ready to go home.

I said, "I have to go now." I started spouting things like, "Please listen to the doctors, so you can get well. Will you do that?" He nodded his head yes. I said again, "I have to go now, but I'll see you soon."

It was Wednesday afternoon, August 21, 2019. In hindsight, don't we all wish we could go back and revisit the last words we have with our loved ones? The sentiment played through my mind constantly after his death, but I've come to realize the words didn't matter. Just being there and getting to spend the last few days with him was enough. It didn't matter what was said. Marty knew it was his time to go.

I was able to hold it together and stay positive, smiling at him the whole time as I was telling him goodbye. As I got up from his bed, and left the room, Marty watched me go. When I got to the hallway, I heard him yell, "Hey!" I ran back into his room. When I got to the door he said, "I love you!" as loud as he could. He was on oxygen and struggling to breathe, yet made the effort to make sure it came out loud and clear. I gave him a gentle hug, trying to say everything in the hug I couldn't say in words. There were no words to express my emotions as I hugged him for the last time. He was a hard-ass with my brothers, but gradually as Marty got older he was the opposite with me. He loved having a daughter.

As an adult, I had developed a strong bond with Marty. I could not imagine life without him in it. It must have taken all of his strength to yell like that, but he wanted to make sure it was the last thing he said to me. It was something he had started doing after Sly died. As I mentioned, he said it at the end of every call and visit. He had never done that before in my life, ever.

As John and I were driving out of the hospital parking garage, my cell phone rang. Mick called to say he was putting Marty in hospice. He said, "If you want to stay, it probably won't be long." I said, "No, I had my goodbye."

I had the strong conviction that it would be Mick and Mary with him at the end. Marty had been like a big brother to my cousin Mary, so it was hard for her as well. If I had stayed, I would have totally lost it. The meltdown I surely would have had would have disrupted an otherwise peaceful environment that Mick and Mary were capable of creating for him at the end. It couldn't have been easy for them either, but I felt they'd be able to stay calm during Marty's last hours.

Marty went downhill quickly, and even told Mick, "This is it" (similar to Sly's comment of, "I guess that's it"). They both had a sense they were at the end and acknowledged it the same way, very simply.

He died on August 24, 2019.

Marty had always said, "When I die, have a party." And that is what we did.

John and I went back to Erie on October 19, 2019. Both Sly and Marty had been cremated; they would both be put in a mausoleum at the cemetery. Their location was outside, in a marbled, engraved space that was part of what looked like a high-end mailbox unit. The cemetery was surrounded by a forest, and the property itself had immaculate landscaping. We had a short ceremony with a few close friends, then we all went to the bar. We drank in Marty's honor.

Two big points to make here:

- Seeing Marty before he died was a gift. I had made the travel arrangements three months earlier, just randomly picking dates, not knowing it would be the last time I'd see him. It truly was a gift from the Universe, so I could have the opportunity to say goodbye in person, and I'm extremely grateful.
- Both parents could have had more time on earth, if they had taken better care of themselves. They died shortly before the pandemic came to our planet, which was a blessing, because the situation would have agitated Sly to no end, and Marty had too many underlying health conditions. It would have been way too much drama for them both.

When I got the phone call from Mick on Saturday, the grief slammed me hard. Marty could be an asshole, but he was my rock. After he died, I drove around Phoenix in my car, by myself screaming as loud as I could. The sounds coming out of me scared me. I sounded like an animal being tortured. That is how painful the grief was. Getting it out via screaming didn't make the pain go away, but I didn't know what else to do. The grief stayed with me for two years. What was surprising to me was how physical it was. Whenever I thought of Marty, who I now referred to as Dad (the power of forgiveness), there was a tangible pain in my chest. I cried a lot during 2020 and 2021. I cried so much I got tired of crying. In hindsight, it was good to get it all out. An exhausting process, though.

My appetite disappeared. I had no interest in food whatsoever, and lost another ten pounds, putting me at 130, which was slightly below the range for my height.

AN: "Ah, this is the opportunity I've been waiting for. The shit that happened to you in Ohio wasn't big enough. This is. The grief is overwhelming you right? I'm here for you girlie when no one else is. Come back. I'm waiting for you with open claws."

ME: "On behalf of Grief and all of my being, I say, 'Hell no, Monster Bitch. I'm grieving, leave me alone. I kicked you out of my life over forty years ago. How pathetic are you trying to come back now? How dare you!'"

People were starting to notice and made comments. I looked thin, but not anorexic, right?

The grief would hang on relentlessly. I couldn't get rid of it, nor could I add any weight back. I saw a grief counselor and read some books on the subject. All of this took place at the height of a global pandemic. I learned that grief is a process. You have to work through it. Don't rush it.

First, the 2017 weight loss I ignored, now this. Questions:

- Was my weight loss an anorexic relapse some forty years later, triggered by grief?
- Was there a genetic switch that had just flicked back on?
- Did my parents' deaths dig up some of the old childhood stuff tied in with Anorexia residue? (For God's sake, hadn't I done enough work to fix all of this?)
- Wait a minute, at 54 years old, aren't I too old for Anorexia?

AN: *"I can suck you in anytime I want. Younger people are easier, but I can get older people too. As a matter of fact, you're never safe from me. I'm in your DNA, so you're fucked. Admit it."*

Was the monster bitch back? No. Maybe. If the Anorexia was full-blown, it would have been a continuous downward spiral on the bathroom scale. It wasn't. I became very aware of the weight loss, and was able to stabilize, and prevent it from going down further. I had all the tools I needed, and knew what to do.

After my parents died, a lot of the childhood stuff resurfaced. I suppose if I was going to relapse into another bout of Anorexia, this would have been it. But something else happened. The death of both my parents brought my journey through Anorexia full circle. I had put the whole ordeal behind me and disassociated myself from it. My rationalization was that it happened to my 16-year old self – that's not *me* anymore. The deaths of my parents brought it up all over again, and forced me to look at it forty years later.

Looking at it through the lens of an older adult, I'm again struck by how vicious an illness it is and how young people are so vulnerable to it. How dangerous it is. And seductive. How critical it is not to underestimate it. I've tried to articulate this message throughout my story.

Once the full circle realization happened, I felt compelled to get my story out. If my Anorexia was hellacious, how much worse is it for others? If what I learned during my hell can help even just one person, then I've done my job as a survivor.

CHAPTER 27
AND THE WINNER IS...
MICHELE, THE ANNIHILATOR

Do I wish Anorexia had never happened to me? I have asked myself that question countless times over the years. The answer used to be *yes*. Anorexia is the worst experience of my life, hands down. Nothing else even comes close. And I was only 16 years old. However, looking back on it now, I realize that from the time I was born, I was destined to get it given the genetic and environmental components to the illness. No way around it. There is nothing I could have done differently, and that realization is a freeing thought.

My Light Bulb Moments have had a powerful combined effect, all of which led to sustained AN recovery for me:

- Surviving my teenage years
- Finishing my education in my 20s
- Intense therapy in my 30s
- Career success in my 40s
- Relationship success in my 50s

It's been a long, tough road. Having Anorexia doesn't automatically equate to a lifetime sentence of food issues, and I know, as a survivor, I need to be vigilant with nutrition, weight, and mental health. When the death of my parents caused a dramatic weight loss, it was time to evaluate, not panic. Re-assess, and stay positive.

As I've said before, Anorexia changed me. I dealt with a very difficult illness at a very young age, how could it not change me? I recognize my weight loss and take accountability for it. I understand that my weight loss could be unhealthy, both physically and psychologically. I know to be able to catch myself so I don't go into the danger zone of Anorexia. Perhaps it took the death of my parents to know I've recovered completely. For that I'm extremely grateful. As of this writing, I'm still 130 lbs. at 5'11", but I'm healthy. Anorexia is a burden I have carried and will continue to carry throughout my life. It reminds me that everyone has a burden. Everyone is dealing with something. Consequently, it is important to be kind to people. Your kindness might make them feel better, even if for a moment. You never know.

It's been said that before we're born, our souls choose the life we're going to have. We choose what we want to accomplish while we're here on earth – what is important to learn, and what we can ignore. We choose our parents. We choose our trials and tribulations. We just can't remember any of it when we get here.

If that is true, then I chose Anorexia, and therefore I have a responsibility to tell my story.

Light Bulb Moment (#15)
I chose Anorexia to see how strong I was.

The result is this book. I feel compelled to tell my story so others who are struggling with Anorexia can see it's possible to get through it and get on with life. And not just get on with life, but have a life of quality. I'm a realist. There are times when life sucks. But there are also beautiful, good, shiny, happy moments and experiences to be had.

In the four decades plus since I had AN, there has been much research and study on Anorexia and eating disorders in general. There is no "one size fits all" cure, but I hope for a cure just the same. I hope enough people in the medical community address the severity of AN as well as the online communities that perpetuate this illness (see: Epilogue).

It blew my mind when I learned that Anorexia could possibly be hereditary. If that is true, I can lose the guilt, blame, and judgment I put on myself. I wasn't defective or weak; it was just something I was born with. Since Sly never talked about her family, I don't know if anyone else had it. I don't know about Marty's side of the family. Most likely someone did, and suffered in silence. That's the irksome part of the journey. I remain optimistic that in today's world of social media, there is enough talk on eating disorders in general to encourage sufferers to speak up. They do not need to be ashamed. They can feel more confident asking for help.

There are so many layers to Anorexia. A 2010 quotation from Michelle Horan RD, LD (www.limrd.com) describes the complexity perfectly: "Eating disorders are not choices; they are psychological diseases that are genetically linked and worsened by stimulus."

Whether you are...

- Suffering in silence...
- In a treatment center...
- Have recovered...
- Have relapsed once or multiple times...

...know that you are capable of annihilating Anorexia. Fight for yourself because you are unique and deserve only the best life has to offer.

AN: "You can be preachy and positive all you want. I am out there. I'm recruiting, hard. I'm so popular! Everyone wants to be thin! Everyone wants to look like the beautiful, perfect people on social media! My #anorexic tag has been viewed over 34 million times on TikTok. Everyone wants me. Perfect is everywhere, and people look at it on their phones constantly. You are delusional if you think you can beat me. I'm the master of the game!"

ME: "Yes, the battle continues between you and me. What you fail to understand with your stupid taunting is that I've learned how to deal with you. I've defeated you completely. Someday there will be a way to get rid of you permanently, for everyone. In the meantime, I have the power, and you know it. You ruin lives, you monster bitch, but you're not going to ruin mine any longer. I win. You lose."

"You're *fat*," Sly said.

ME: "No Sly, I'm not fat. 'Fat' is a label. A label means nothing. I'm me and I've learned how to be strong. Annihilating Anorexia means everything and I did it. Shame on you for not helping me, but it's okay. I'm me and I did it."

I became The Annihilator and so can *you.*

EPILOGUE: THE 1-2 PUNCH

I was hospitalized with Anorexia in 1981. I wrote this book in 2021.

Has any progress been made in the last forty years? Is there any good news for Anorexia's victims – past, present and future?

Yes and No.

Yes, in that there is much more awareness concerning mental illness in young people, including Anorexia. Awareness is a good thing. However, in my opinion, there is still a stigma of shame to eating disorders in general. Why? Because any kind of mental health issue is still considered by society in general as a weakness. There is still ignorance. The "Why can't you just eat something" or "You're just doing this for attention."

Young people deal with:

- Academic and Athletic Pressure
- Peer Pressure
- Unrealistic Parental Expectations

And, now guess what? Mental illness is being bolstered by a couple of key partners in crime. The 1-2 Punch of:

- A Global Pandemic
- Social Media

During the global pandemic, kids (and people in general) didn't get do all of the things they love to do. In an effort to stay occupied, and for lack of anything better to do, they went to social media. Combined, it's a destructive 1-2 punch to the mental health and well-being of youth. Isolation encourages eating disorders. 30 million (20 million women and 10 million men) Americans have struggled with an eating disorder. 150 million (half of the U.S. population) know someone with an eating disorder. The following are just a sampling of national news sources that have covered the 1-2 punch:

PUNCH #1 – THE PANDEMIC

CNN: Hospitalization for eating disorders grew in the pandemic. The problem isn't over, experts say, **November 7, 2022:**

From the spring of 2020 – when most Covid-19 restrictions/lockdowns were first put in place — through spring 2021, the number of eating disorder inpatient admissions about doubled. This number rose to its peak in April 2021. (Madeline Holcomb)

People Magazine: "I'm Sick of Living Like This" America's Got Talent Finalist Jackie Evancho's Struggle with Anorexia, **July 18, 2022:**

Evancho first sought treatment for Anorexia at age 17, but it's been an ongoing health hurdle. "Each year I was watching it just get worse and worse and worse – and then the pandemic hit," she says. "The urge to restrict what I'm eating, on top of eating because I'm bored, and panic because I have this distorted view of myself in the mirror…it made everything really difficult. There weren't distractions during COVID."

The Defender [Children's Health News and Views]: Eating Disorders Among Teen Girls Doubled During Pandemic, CDC Study Shows, February 22, 2022:

Emergency room visits for eating disorders among 12- to 17-year-old girls doubled during the coronavirus pandemic, according to new research from the U.S. Centers for Disease Control and Prevention – a troubling existing trend that was likely worsened by the stress of living through the prolonged crisis.

Wall Street Journal: *Eating Disorders Surge in Kids*, June 22, 2021:

Tracy Richmond, Director of the Eating Disorder Program at Boston Children's Hospital, recently finished a study accepted for publication in the *Journal of Adolescent Health* showing hospitalization rates of eating disorder patients at Boston Children's more than tripled in the pandemic, with the in-patient numbers rising from three or four to more than 10 and as many as 16 at the time.

"Patients who come in are just really sick," Dr. Richmond said. "Some have lost as much as 50% of their body weight."

Eating Recovery Center, a private network of 30 centers in seven states, says it received about 2,000 more new patient calls in the first two months of 2021, a 90% increase over the same period in 2020.

There was no wait list for out-patient treatment at the Eating Disorders Center at Children's Mercy Kansas City before the pandemic. Now the wait is about six months.

Wall Street Journal: **The Pandemic's Toll on Teen Mental Health, June 11, 2021:**

Lockdowns and school closures have led to greater incidences of obesity and eating disorders, according to experts at the Stanford Children's Health network.

The proportion of children seeking emergency mental-health services who required immediate hospitalization, including for eating disorders, rose 75% in 2020 compared with 2019.

PUNCH #2 – SOCIAL MEDIA

Wall Street Journal: Eating-Disorder Videos Slip Past TikTok's Blocks, **September 27, 2022:**

Naomi Sanders tried to set up her TikTok account so she wouldn't see videos about eating disorders, but she says they're impossible to avoid. I still see posts related to eating disorders on my feed at least three times a day, says the 15-year-old high-school sophomore from Bellingham, Wash., who's been struggling with unhealthy eating habits since middle school.

Other videos Naomi finds troubling are ones about recovering from an eating disorder. She says people often show photos of themselves at their thinnest and mention how much weight they lost. Naomi says those videos can spark competitiveness in teens like her – and sow doubts about how sick they themselves really were, since they didn't lose as much weight as the people in the videos.

Wall Street Journal: When Boys Fall Prey to Eating Disorders, November 16, 2021:

Griffin Henry's whole life revolved around baseball. Mr. Henry searched Instagram for workout videos and posts about pre-and-post-workout meals. As the weight came off, Mr. Henry began to look cut. As her son lost more weight...his mom, Linsey Henry, noticed, even though he tried to hide it by wearing baggy clothes.

...Mr Henry's mother took him to a doctor who observed his heart rate was below 50 beats a minute. The doctor sent him to Children's Mercy Hospital, where Dr. Voss diagnosed him with Anorexia Nervosa. After two weeks in the hospital, Mr. Henry spent six weeks at a residential treatment center to gain weight. The program didn't allow personal devices. "The best part of treatment was not being on my phone," he [Mr. Henry] said.

Doctors and university researchers say social media is a contributing factor in boys' body issues. They experience body-image comparisons on social media just as girls do. Social media algorithms also push exercise videos and posts that research has found can lead to disordered eating.

Wall Street Journal: Facebook Knows Instagram is Toxic for Teen Girls, Its Research Shows, September 15, 2021:

In 2020, at the height of a worldwide pandemic, teenager Anastasia started seeing a therapist. She had developed an eating disorder, and had a clear idea of what led to it: her time on Instagram.

"When I went on Instagram, all I saw were images of chiseled bodies, perfect abs and women doing 100 burpees in 10 minutes. I had to live with my eating disorder for five years, and people on Instagram are still suffering." Instagram has an inherent obsessive quality about it. It is often used as a measure of popularity. It becomes important, almost addictive, to know how many followers you have, and is that more or less than your friends? Users know it's not healthy to spend excessive time on Instagram, but they can't stop. Too much peer pressure.

These stories are truly frightening. If you're struggling with Anorexia or any kind of eating disorder, tell someone. Anyone. Tell them you're scared. Tell them you need help. Don't let the patterns get so ingrained that you can't even talk about it with someone. Based on the statistics above, everyone is either struggling with an eating disorder, or they know someone who is. Everyone.

Back to the progress question: Yes or No? Here's the No part. No, because there isn't a cure for Anorexia yet. Perhaps someday there will be a way to screen, to determine genetic pre-disposition. What if checking for eating disorders, depression, and anxiety was part of a routine physical, along with temperature and blood pressure? What if everyone was encouraged to speak freely about mental issues? And commended for doing so? If the potential for Anorexia was great, then a course of treatment prescribed to prevent the person from getting Anorexia in the first place? Prevention would end so much suffering.

I found a way to beat the monster bitch that is Anorexia. Otherwise I'd be dead. It truly is a matter of life or death with this illness. I chose to live, even though it was *so hard*. Again, if there is anything

I've learned in my healing journey, it's that Anorexia is a complex, insidious illness. It's not surprising there's no cure for Anorexia because there is no definitive answer on what causes it. Yet. The blueprint is different for everyone. Everyone's struggle is unique, which is why it is so important to bring awareness.

Awareness is key to Annihilating Anorexia.

ACKNOWLEDGMENTS

Sharing my story publicly without the support of my two brothers would have been impossible. Mick and Mark, thank you for being the first to read my manuscript and for your encouragement, not only for my book, but also throughout my life.

A heartfelt thank you to Leah and Terry, my lifelong friends who offered valuable suggestions that made my book exponentially better. Also, to my dear friend Shari, who held space for me on "our" mountain when the writing and remembering got really hard.

A loving thank you to my husband John, who was my biggest cheerleader throughout the entire three-year process of researching and writing my book.

A sincere thank you to the health care professionals who helped me get well in 1981. And a grateful thank you again in 2020 for providing hard copies of all my medical records.

To the talented team at The Paper House, an enthusiastic thank you for bringing my book to life and for your sensitivity on the subject matter.

HELP RESOURCES

National Association of Anorexia Nervosa and Associated
Disorders (ANAD)
www.anad.org

National Eating Disorders Association (NEDA)
www.nationaleatingdisorders.org

National Alliance for Eating Disorders ("The Alliance")
www.allianceforeatingdisorders.com

Milton Keynes UK
Ingram Content Group UK Ltd.
UKHW020726030823
426269UK00014B/635

9 781088 178546